Humanism

Humanism

Finding

Meaning

in the

Word

Nicolas Walter

PB Prometheus Books

59 John Glenn Drive
Amherst, New York 14228-2197

Published 1998 by Prometheus Books

Originally published as *Humanism: What's in the Word*. Rationalist Press Association, London, England. Copyright © 1997 Rationalist Press Association.

02 01 00 99 98   5 4 3 2 1

Library of Congress Cataloging-in-Publication Data

Walter, Nicolas, 1934–
    Humanism : finding meaning in the Word / Nicolas Walter.
        p.   cm.
    Originally published: London, England : Rationalist Press Association, c1997.
    Includes bibliographical references and index.
    ISBN 1–57392–209–9 (alk. paper)
    1. Humanism. I. Title.
BL2747.6.W35   1998
144—dc21
                                                            98–14693
                                                            CIP

Printed in the United States of America on acid-free paper.

Contents

Preface

The tradition of what is now called humanism is very old, but the words *humanism* and *humanist* are rather new, and their general use by nonreligious freethinkers is quite recent. The object of this book is to tell the story not of the tradition but of the words, from their original appearances a few centuries ago to their eventual adoption by the freethought movement during the present century. The motive is to explore the various meanings of *humanism* in the past so as to clarify the origins and development of what is now known as the humanist movement. The hope is to help future discussion become better informed, and better behaved. A discussion of the name rather than the thing—nominalism rather than realism—may have practical as well as theoretical significance.

"What's in a name?" asked Juliet. A great deal, as she learnt, at the cost of her life. What's in the word *humanism*? Not so much, of course, but still quite a lot. The tale of its changing fortunes should be interesting and instructive, and can be both amusing and annoying. At times it seems to exist in a fantasy world of Charles Dickens or Lewis Carroll. In the first of *The Posthumous Papers of the Pickwick Club* (1836), Mr. Blotton excused his use of the word *humbug* by saying that "he had used the word in its Pickwickian sense." "When I use a word," said Humpty Dumpty in *Through the Looking Glass, and What Alice Found There* (1871), "it means just what I choose it to mean—neither more nor less." *Humanism* has often been used in a Pickwickian sense, to mean just what the user chooses it to mean. A. N. Whitehead wrote a fascinating book called *Adventures of Ideas* (1933)—one of which was "The Humanitarian Ideal"; ideas are expressed in words, and adventures of words have a fascination of their own, as they and their meanings twist and turn.

This book is based on the study of a large number of publications of all kinds held by the national humanist organizations or in national reference libraries in Britain. Thanks are due to the humanists in all senses, at all levels, in all places, who have produced and preserved this material, provided time and space to inquirers, exchanged ideas and information, offered comments and corrections, given professional and personal assistance, and individually and collectively acted in the spirit of humanity.

Thanks are due especially to the humanist organizations which supported this work, to Heiner Becker and Christine Walter who helped with it, and to the American colleagues who have republished it.

Nicolas Walter

Introduction

The words *humanist* and *humanism* obviously have a connection with the words *human* and *humanity*, translated from the Latin *humanus* and *humanitas*, derived from *homo/hominis* (man), and cognate with *humus* (earth). But what the connection ought to be in theory isn't always obvious, and what the connection has been in practice is often surprising. Many people have been called or have called themselves humanists without any clear indication or understanding of what this means.

All the uses of *humanism* relate in some way to the *human* and to *humanity*—positively, by affirming or approving of some aspects of human nature or interest, or negatively, by negating or disapproving of something other than humanity, such as nature or the universe, animality or barbarity, God or the state, science or society. The word has been used in ways which are religious or irreligious, historical or logical, descriptive or prescriptive. One feature common to almost all of them is that it has been a "hurrah word," used melioratively to express vague approval rather than clear definition; all too often, *humanist* has meant little more than *nice* and *humanism* little more than *niceness.* Conversely, they have sometimes been used pejoratively with insulting meanings of *softness* or *sentimentality.*

A frequent feature is the retrospective application of *humanist* to people and of *humanism* to movements that didn't use the term. An occasional feature is the denial of the terms to people and movements that did use them. Such semantic confusion has often made it difficult to know what the words do mean in theory, which makes it all the more important to discover what they have meant in practice.

First Words

The words *humanist* and *humanism* first appeared five and two centuries ago respectively, in Italy and Germany respectively, not so much as titles of ideological systems but rather as labels in scholarly discourse and educational debate. They first merged and then they acquired more and more quite different meanings, until during the twentieth century they eventually became the most common terms for the freethought ideology which combines rationalist, secularist, ethicist, atheist, naturalist views of the universe and of the human species. The process of development is generally supposed to be fairly simple and straightforward, but it was actually complex and confused, and as a result the current situation is frequently uncertain and unclear.

To begin at the beginning, two of the basic ideas of humanism—concerning our relationship with the world, and concerning our relationship with one another—were neatly expressed in two texts from the dawn of European civilization more than two thousand years ago. One is the saying of the fifth-century Greek philosopher Protagoras, "that man is the measure of all things"—*pantôn khrêmatôn anthrôpon metron einai* (quoted from his lost book *On Truth* by philosophers from Plato and Aristotle to Sextus Empiricus and Diogenes Laertius).

The other is the remark in a play by the second-century Roman dramatist Terence (Publius Terentius Afer) by a character who says, "I am a man; I think nothing human strange to me"—*Homo sum; humani nil a me alienum puto* (*Heauton timorumenos*, "The Self-Tormentor," adapted from the fourth-century Greek dramatist Menander).

The latter idea was put more earnestly by the Stoic philosophers, who established the first permanent tradition which taught the universal brotherhood of all human beings. This was later summarized in the *Natural History* of the first-century Roman writer, the elder Pliny (Gaius Plinius Secundus), in what could be called the principle of religious humanism, as rendered in the first English translation by Philemon Holland in 1601: "A god unto a man is he that helpeth a man. and this is the true and direct way to everlasting glorie" *Deus est mortali juvare mortalem, et haec ad aeternam gloriam via* (*Historia Naturalis* 2.5). And the first-century Roman politician and philosopher Seneca (Lucius Annaeus Seneca) concluded his dialogue *On Anger* with the plea that "while we draw breath, while we are among men, let us cultivate humanity"—*colamus humanitatem* (*De ira* 3.43).

The most basic principle of humanism—concerning our relationship with ourselves—was also expressed in antiquity. In Greece the highest cultural and moral ideal was *paideia* (education or cultivation, but more than either). This was transmitted to Rome through some of the "middle" Stoic thinkers—especially the second-century Panaetius of Rhodes and the first-century Posidonius of Rhodes—who occasionally rendered it as *andreia* (manliness); and this was translated into Latin as *virtus* (manliness), and also as *humanitas* (humanity). In particular the first-century Roman orator and writer, Cicero (Marcus Tullius Cicero), who read Panaetius and studied with Posidonius, proclaimed in his treatise *On the Orator* that the orator, the fully educated man, "should be perfect in every part of humanity"—*in omni parte humanitatis . . . perfectum esse debere* (*De oratore* 1.71).

Cicero had great influence in both ancient and medieval Europe, but his ideal was soon narrowed from educated *humanity* in general to *educated* humans in particular. In the second century C.E. the Roman writer Aulus Gellius insisted in his *Attic Nights* that *humanitas* meant not so much love of human beings as the cultivation of one's own humanity—not *philanthrôpia* ("a kind of amiability and benevolence toward all men indiscriminately") but *paideia* ("education and learning in the fine arts"); those who pursued *humanitas* in this sense were "most humanest"—*maxime humanissimi* (*Noctes Atticae*, 13.17). It was called *humanitas* because it was possessed only by human beings, and in theory it was available to all human beings; but in practice it was clearly restricted to an intellectual if not a social elite, and this is what it came to mean.

Humanity in this sense was equated with *Romanness* (*romanitas*), and opposed to *barbarism*, which meant first the quality of not being Greek and then the quality not so much of not being human in the philosophical sense as of not being civilized in the cultural sense. And in this sense *humanity* survived the coming of Christianity and later became one of the cultural ideals of western Europe, opposed to intellectual *barbarism*, as represented by pedantic and dogmatic Scholasticism. This is where the *humanists* and *humanism* came from.

On the other side of the world, in ancient China, the cultural and moral ideal of the fifth-century sage Confucius (Kung Fu-ze) and his fourth-century successor Mencius (Meng-ze) was *ren* (humanness)—again the theoretical attribute of the complete human being, again applied in practice only to the educated elite. In modern Chinese, the word for *human* or *humanity* is still *ren*, and humanism is *ren-wen-zhu-yi* or *ren-ben-zhu-yi* (study of or devotion to human principle). And in ancient India, one of the words for the suppressed stream of skeptical materialism in Hindu thought was *Lokayata* (found among the people).

So the basic principles of humanism—the recognition of the equal humanness of all humans, and the cultivation of the essential humanity of the individual human—have existed as long as human civilization has existed, and have been expressed around the world in words meaning *man*. (These words cover both sexes in all the ancient languages.) It was perhaps only a matter of time for *humanism* the word to be invented for humanism the thing, though it was in fact a long time before this happened.

It is odd that *anthropism*, the Greek equivalent of *humanism*, has hardly ever been used in the same sense. Whereas *humanismus* didn't appear in ancient or medieval Latin, *anthrôpismos* did appear in ancient Greek; it was used by Diogenes Laertius, the philosophical biographer of the third century C.E., in a statement attributed to the fifth-century philosopher Aristippus of Cyrene—"It is better to be impoverished than uneducated: the one lacks wealth, the other lacks *humanity*"—*anthrôpismos* (*Lives and Opinions of the Eminent Philosophers* 2.70). It also survived in medieval Greek and into modern Greek, where *anthrôpismos* is now an occasional alternative to *houmanismos* for the various meanings of *humanism*. But its only appearance in other languages seems to have been in the pejorative sense used by the German biologist and monist, Ernst Haeckel, where *anthropism* means the false elevation of humanity above the universe.

Wild Words

Words are wild things, like books. The Roman grammarian Terentianus Maurus said, "Books have their fates"—*Habent sua fata libelli* (*De letteris, syllabis*, etc.). And the Roman poet Horace (Quintus Horatius Flaccus) said, "And once released a word flies off without recall"—*Et semel emissum volat inrevocabile verbum* (*Epistolae* 18). He was echoing Homer's phrase "winged words" (*epea pteroenta*). When a book is published, it breaks away and leads its own life—as may be seen from the Bible to *The Satanic Verses*; and when a word is coined, it too breaks away and leads its own life—as will be seen from *humanist* and *humanism*.

Attempts to control books and words almost never succeed; the censorship of books and the regulation of words almost always fail. Churches and states suppress books, and academies and dictionaries condemn words; but the suppressors and condemners die, and the books and the words live on. The story of the vitality of books is very well known; the story of the similar vitality of words is less well known. The Accademia della Crusca and the Académie Française tried to control the Italian and French languages, but the Italians and the French took no more notice of rules about their words than about their deeds. The Greek and Norwegian authorities tried to impose official languages in their countries during the early twentieth century, but the Greeks and the Norwegians went on speaking their popular vernaculars. The English authorities tried to ban Welsh and the Turkish authorities try to ban Kurdish, but the Welsh continued and the Kurds continue to speak their native languages. Samuel Johnson's and Noah Webster's dictionaries of the British and American varieties of English tried but failed to standardize the language, and later dictionaries ended by recording its enormous variations.

It is important to learn from these lessons, but it is easy to forget them. Too many members of the organized humanist movement, who call themselves *humanists* and call for *humanism*, are too much inclined to make the mistake of trying to appropriate these words, to claim them as being "our own," and to restrict their use to our sense (assuming, of course, that we agree about "our" sense).

This happens not only in theoretical discussion but in practical action. At the founding congress of the International Humanist and Ethical Union (IHEU) in 1952, Rudolf Dreikurs of the American Humanist Association made the following statement:

> One of the greatest obstacles which organized Humanism encounters is the ambiguity of the term *Humanism*. The semantic confusion surrounding this term is well understandable from a historical point of view. Too many meanings were implied in this word during the past centuries. Many of them will have to be discarded before Humanism will be generally understood in the way we understand it.

After several decades of discussion, IHEU eventually issued a *Minimum Statement* to be accepted by its affiliated organizations. The text, which was drafted by the Norwegian leader Levi Fragell and adopted by the IHEU Board at Prague in 1991, and amended by the addition of a middle sentence by the IHEU Board at Mexico City in 1996, is now the official basic definition of *humanism*:

> Humanism is a democratic and ethical life stance which affirms that human beings have the right and responsibility to give meaning and shape to their own lives. [It stands for the building of a more humane society through an ethics based on human and other natural values in a spirit of reason and free inquiry through human capabilities.] It is not theistic, and it does not accept supernatural views of reality.

Individual members of the humanist movement have also unofficially complained about any qualification of *humanism*, and especially about any which associates it with religion. They have specifically condemned such phrases as *religious humanism* or *Christian humanism* or *humanistic Judaism* as being contradictory, and such phrases as *secular humanism* or *scientific humanism* or *ethical humanism* as being confusing. They have even accused other users of *humanism* of stealing it.

This approach is surely both impracticable and undesirable. Many if not most of the people who have called themselves or have been called humanists at any time would reject some if not most of the dozen propositions contained in either version of the *Minimum Statement*. The origins of *humanism* are so contradictory and confusing that it is often meaningless on its own. The various forms of *religious humanism* may puzzle both religious and nonreligious people, but they make sense to religious humanists themselves. Because of the survival of such versions of humanism, *scientific humanism* is still a useful term to describe a nonreligious view of humanity and the world based on scientific principles and tending toward social and political action. For the same reason, *secular humanism* is still a useful term to describe a nonreligious view of humanity and the world based on sec-ular principles. Similarly, *ethical humanism* is still a useful term for a positive view of morality based on naturalistic principles, and *rationalist humanism* may still be a useful term to describe a nonreligious view of humanity based on reason rather than emotion.

Anyway, it is only half a century since we took over words which for several centuries had already been used by other kinds of people with other kinds of meanings, so that we may just as well be accused of stealing them as anyone else. To take a revealing example, Margaret Knight's *Humanist Anthology* (1961) included no items containing the words until 1955, three-quarters of the way through the book and only six years before it was published, although they had been used for many years before then.

The facts are that, while *humanism* happens to be the word we now use, it isn't "our own"; that it has been, is being, and will be used by many other people in many other ways; that most of its senses have actually involved religion; that many of its nonreligious senses are unclear without qualification; that all viable senses of a word are equally valid; that semantic dogmatism and verbal authoritarianism are quite alien to what most of us understand by being humanist or supporting humanism; that words can't be "stolen"; and that neither we nor anyone else could control the words even if we wished to. As Ludwig Wittgenstein said, "the meaning of a word is the way in which it is used," and as Rudolf Lotze said, "things are what they are known as"; among the most interesting things about *humanism* are the way in which it has been used and what it has been known as.

Last Words

It must be recorded at the start that there is no single reliable account of this subject, and hardly any authoritative material, except in a few variable monographs on various aspects. Standard reference books give little help; the *Oxford English Dictionary* gives only five meanings each for *humanist* and *humanism*, several of which it gets wrong. Standard textbooks are no better and often much worse. No publications about or by the humanist movement have yet dealt satisfactorily with the historical semantics of its key words. (See the note on pages 135–36.)

Even the many previous attempts by bibliographers and librarians simply to classify the various changing meanings of *humanism* have been unsuccessful. Alan Bullock accordingly opened his book *The Humanist Tradition in the West* (1985) with a discussion of the meanings of *humanist* and *humanism*, commenting that they are "words that no one has ever succeeded in defining to anyone else's satisfaction, protean words which mean very different things to different people and leave lexicographers and encyclopaedists with a feeling of exasperation and frustration," and concluding that humanism is "not a school of thought or a philosophical doctrine, but a broad tendency, a dimension of thought and belief, a continuing debate." Gloria K. Fiero opened her multivolume educational history of *The Humanistic Tradition* (1981–1995) by defining this generally as "humankind's cultural legacy—the sum total of the significant ideas and achievements handed down from generation to generation," and especially as "the creative legacy referred to collectively as the humanities" (literature, philosophy, history, art). Tony Davies began his short educational survey of *Humanism* (1997) by aiming "Towards a Definition of Humanism," but noting that "humanism is a word with a very complex history and an unusually wide range of possible meanings and contexts" and emphasizing "the vertiginously proliferating and often contradictory senses attributed to the word," and ended by returning to "the word," but refusing to choose any single sense, confusing what senses there are, and looking forward to further "new humanisms." None of these authors, by the way, accepts our sense of *humanism*; Bullock rejects it, Fiero omits it, Davies evades it.

The proper way to understand how our particular sense(s) of *humanism* and *humanist* arose is to trace all the many meanings of the words as they have actually arisen. This is the first attempt to do so based on a thorough examination of the relevant source material, though it has been kept as brief and clear as possible, and further research would uncover many more examples of changing usage.

Throughout this book it is worth remembering seven points:

1. Words expressing the meanings of terms are generally italicized.

2. The word *man* normally includes both sexes.

3. Such terms as *antiquity* and the *Middle Ages*, the *Renaissance* and the *Enlightenment* weren't used at the times, but were applied retrospectively and sometimes misleadingly by later generations.

4. Most of the people who are now considered as humanists didn't call themselves humanists, and many of the people who have called themselves humanists aren't now considered as humanists.

5. This study is mainly concerned with those people who did call themselves humanists and with those ideas which were called humanism at the time.

6. There is an inevitable bias toward material in English and events in Britain, although most of the developments discussed occurred in other languages and other places.

7. References have been given as briefly as possible; interested readers will have to follow the author by studying the whole of the items quoted.

Humanists, Humanities, Humanisms

The words *humanism* and *humanist* weren't used in so-called antiquity, although they have often been used to describe certain aspects of the civilizations of ancient Greece and Rome and also of ancient China and India, and as we have seen words meaning *man* were already used then for some of these aspects. Neither were they used during the so-called Middle Ages between the ancient and modern periods. They each emerged separately in the cultural discourse or debate of modern Europe.

The First Humanists

The word *humanist* was first used during the so-called Renaissance without any ideological meaning at all.* It appeared in northern Italy

---

*The standard account is Augusto Campana's article on "The Origin of the Word *Humanist*" in the *Journal of the Warburg and Courtauld Institutes* 9 (1946).

in the late fifteenth century as a technical term in the world of university education. Some manuscripts in Latin and Italian dating from the 1490s have been found in such academic centers as Bologna and Pisa (centers of Aristotelian rather than Platonic studies), listing *humanista* or *umanista* alongside other kinds of specialist—*alchimista* (chemistry), *artista* (arts), *canonista* (canon law), *jurista* (jurisprudence), *legista* (civil law), and so on—probably copying student slang for members of the various faculties.

The term derived from medieval ideas about ancient Rome. Cicero's cultural ideal of *humanitas* was considered to involve "the art of living well and blessedly through learning and instruction in the fine arts," beginning with language and literature. West European scholars during the late Middle Ages interpreted this to mean the study of the languages and literature of ancient Rome and later of ancient Greece. From the early fifteenth century specialization in this area was therefore called *studia humanitatis* (studies of humanity) or *litterae humaniores* (more human letters), concentrating on human matters, especially the classics—by contrast with *studia divinitatis* (studies of divinity) and *litterae sacrae* (holy letters), concentrating on religious matters such as Scripture and theology—and by the end of the fifteenth century the specialists in this area became known as *humanists*.

These first humanists were scholars, teachers, and students who continued, revived, and extended the classical tradition, who specialized in grammar, rhetoric, poetics, history, and moral philosophy as found in classical authors, and who worked as discoverers, editors, and translators of classical texts. They didn't venture into such other areas as theology, law, art, music, medicine, natural philosophy (science), or logic and metaphysics (technical philosophy), which were all the territory of other faculties. They didn't see themselves as the agents of change—far from wishing to go forward, if anything, they wished to go backward—but, despite themselves, their cultural nostalgia gave a significant impetus to cultural progress.

Positively, by preserving or reviving the texts of antiquity they preserved or revived the ideas of antiquity, and they were even some-times tempted by pagan religion or by skeptical or naturalistic aspects of ancient philosophy and science; negatively, by upgrading the ideas of antiquity they implicitly or explicitly downgraded the ideas of what they called the "Middle Age" between the ancient and modern worlds, especially Scholastic philosophy and science, and sometimes orthodox Christianity itself; historically, by treating all ancient docu-ments equally critically they began the rational treatment of biblical as well as classical texts, a process which would eventually destroy the unique authority of Judaeo-Christian Scripture; generally, because their approach to scholarship prevailed, they unwittingly laid some of the cultural foundations for the world we have lived in ever since. (In a similar way, the Protestant Reformation, which was intended to reform and revive Christianity, initiated its division and decline.)

The original narrow sense of *humanist* as a specialist in Latin and Greek language and literature—which is still used as a technical term in the scholarly study of the Renaissance—soon spread through and beyond Italy. It appeared in print in both Latin and Italian during the early sixteenth century, the best-known instance being a reference to "grammatici" and "umanisti" in Ludovico Ariosto's *Satires* (1534), and it soon appeared in other languages.

Humaniste is first found in French in 1552; Michel de Montaigne used it in the second edition of his *Essais* (1582), remarking in the essay on prayer, "That fault of theologians writing too humanly is seen more often than that other fault of humanists writing too untheologi-cally" (1.15). However, the word wasn't accepted by the Académie Française until 1718. *Humanista* appeared in Spanish in 1614, when it was used in a poem by Miguel de Cervantes; and in the second part of his novel *Don Quixote* (1615), when a wandering scholar was asked about his pursuits, his profession and studies, he "replied that his pro-fession was to be a humanist, his pursuits and studies to compose books to give to the press" (*Segunda parte del ingenioso cavallero don Quixote de La Mancha*, chapter 22). *Humanist* wasn't used in German until the eighteenth century, and wasn't included in the Grimm brothers' *Deutsches Wörterbuch* as late as 1877.

Humanist is first found in English in 1589, in the translation of *The Georgiks* [*sic*] *of Publius Virgilius Maro* by "A. F." (Abraham Fleming); the preface "To the Reader whatsoever" apologized for the defects of the translation to "weake Grammatists" and "courtly Humanists." And *A New Discourse of a Stale Subject, called The Metamorphosis of Ajax* (1596) by "Misacmos" (John Harington)—the first published proposal for a water closet—echoed Montaigne's epigram with the remark: "I might repute him as a good humanist, but I should ever doubt him for a good divine." In *Of the Proficience and Advancement of Learning* (1605), Francis Bacon referred to such rivals of physicians as "antiquaries, poets, humanists, statesmen, merchants, divines"; in the Latin version of *De dignitate et augmentis scientiarum* (1623), the list was given as "poets, antiquaries, critics, rhetoricians, statesmen, divines," so "humanists" presumably meant "critics" and "rhetoricians."

But by then the word had also acquired a wider meaning altogether. In *An Itinerary . . . Containing His Ten Yeeres Travell* (1617), Fynes Moryson said in the section "Of Precepts for Travellers":

> I profess to write especially in this place to the Humanist, I mean him that affects the knowledge of State affaires, Histories, Cosmography, and the like. . . . As an Orator and Poet must haue some skill in all Sciences, so the Humanist must haue some knowledge of all things which fall into practise and discourse.

Humanist was nevertheless rather narrowly defined by Samuel Johnson in *A Dictionary of the English Language* (1755) as "a philologer; a grammarian." It was still narrowly defined by Noah Webster in *An American Dictionary of the English Language* (1841) as "a professor of grammar and rhetoric" and "a philologist," though also as "one versed in the knowledge of human nature." (Lexicographers are often far from harmless drudges who prefer the easy path of repeating the precedents of other dictionaries to the hard road of recording the actual usage of real people.)

The first publication in English to use the word in its title was *The Humanist*, one of many general magazines published in London during the mid-eighteenth century, which took it in the broad rather than any restricted sense. The anonymous editor and main contributor was Patrick Delany, an eccentric Irish clergyman and writer who was then living in England. He wrote in its first weekly issue (March 26, 1757) that he disliked the titles of magazines like *The Rambler* or *The Adventurer*:

> I must confess that the title of HUMANIST seems to me much more agreeable to the nature and reason of a paper, calculated to recommend every thing that is amiable and beneficent in human nature, than any which writings of that kind have hitherto taken up. . . . The title of HUMANIST is clear of all these objections; and implies neither more nor less, than that it interests itself in all the concerns of human nature: at least, a paper undertaken upon that view, is sufficiently justified in assuming that title. How far it will answer in the event, experience only can evince.

The paper's motto was the well-known quotation from Terence. It was advertised as "a new paper called—THE HUMANIST":

> Which means not only amusement, like the rest of its contemporaries, but likewise something more than mere amusement; and is calculated to convey some little useful and entertaining knowledge of various kinds, historical, classical, natural, moral, and *now-and-then* a *little religion*, into the readers' mind.

It contained miscellaneous articles and letters, none clearly relating to its title—except perhaps for an attack on "those who degraded their humanity" by horse-docking (May 21, 1757). In the event it did not answer; the fifteenth issue (July 2, 1757) announced that it would cease publication for four months, but it never resumed publication.

No other periodical used the title for a century, when a German-language paper in the United States did so in 1854 and a Dutch paper did so in 1881.

Toward Humanism

The word *humanist* continued to be used, but not by or for those who broke with the past in what is now called the humanist tradition, as manifested in the scientific and intellectual revolutions of the sixteenth and seventeenth centuries, or the so-called Enlightenment of the seventeenth and eighteenth centuries, or the political and social revolutions of the eighteenth and nineteenth centuries.

It was not adopted by the French *libertins* or *esprits forts*, the British freethinkers or deists, the Scottish moralists or French *philosophes*, the British Utilitarians or American Transcendentalists. Immanuel Kant and Denis Diderot both put *humanity* at the center of their respective philosophies, but neither thought to call himself a *humanist*. Thomas Paine referred to "the religion of humanity"—in the seventh number of *The Crisis* (November 21, 1778)—but when a sect was founded on this principle, in France in 1797, they were called not *humanists* but *theophilanthropists*. Johann Bernhard Basedow followed similar principles in his educational reforms in eighteenth-century Germany, but his followers were called not *humanists* but *philanthropinists*.

Other German intellectuals of the time, including J. W. von Goethe and Friedrich Schiller, developed a romantic cult of the "idea" or the "ideal" of *mankind* or *humanity*. One of the group's publicists, Johann Gottfried Herder, deliberately changed the name of this ideal in his two multivolume works—from *Ideen zur Philosophie der Geschichte der Menschheit* (Ideas toward the Philosophy of the History of Mankind) in 1784–1791 to *Briefe zu Beförderung der Humanität* (Letters toward the Promotion of Humanity) in 1793–1797. Another was Wilhelm von Humboldt, later the founder of the Prussian educational system, who in 1797 wrote *Ueber den Geist der Menschheit* (On the Spirit of Humanity) and in 1792 wrote in *Ideen zu einem Versuch die Grenzen der Wirksamkeit des Staats zu bestimmen*—published in 1852 and translated as *The Sphere and Duties of Government* (1854)—the sentence quoted by John Stuart Mill as the epigraph for *On Liberty* (1859):

> The grand, leading principle, towards which every argument unfolded
> in these pages directly converges, is the absolute and essential impor-
> tance of human development in its richest diversity.

But none of these writers called himself a *humanist*. Similarly, in nine-
teenth-century France, Pierre Leroux proposed and Auguste Comte
founded a "Religion of Humanity," but their followers were generally
called not *humanists* but *humanitarians* and *positivists* respectively.

In fact, in the various battles between ancients and moderns for
four centuries the people who called themselves *humanists* almost
always belonged to the ancients, looking back to the increasingly dis-
tant Greeks and Romans of antiquity, to the study of their increasingly
lifeless languages and their increasingly unfamiliar literature, and
looking forward to the preservation of the traditional education of the
intellectual elite. Symbolically, early humanists opposed the new
invention of printing, preferring the more "human" tradition of manuscripts, and despised writing in vernacular languages, preferring Latin
and Greek. Similarly, later humanists mostly belonged to the nonsci-
entific culture defined in C. P. Snow's Rede Lecture *Two Cultures and
the Scientific Revolution* (1959). For a long time, indeed, humanists
belonged not to the future but to the past.

Yet *humanist* was a useful word, despite the early confusion about
its meaning. It isn't surprising that it survived. What is surprising is
that it took so long for the word *humanist* to be joined by the word
humanism.

The Humanities

Meanwhile the Latin terms used for the university subject of the original *humanists* soon led to the use of the terms *humanity* or *humanis-
tics* and then *humanities* in several languages to describe the academic
study first of Latin and Greek, then more generally of arts, languages,

literature, history, philosophy, and finally of virtually everything which is not religious or scientific, technical or vocational.

The old terms survived in such universities as Oxford, where the classical course is still called *litterae humaniores*, or in Scotland, where professors of Latin are still called professors of humanity. But the new term *humanities* became almost universal in the relevant faculties of other universities around the world. Eventually teachers and students of the humanities in this broad sense, not only in universities but also in schools, were often called *humanists*, regardless of whether they knew any Greek or Latin, or indeed whether they had any particular interest in humanity.

But the words *humanist* and *humanities*, which were applied in the ways described to people and to activities, required a word for the ideas which were possessed by such people and which inspired such activities.

The First Humanism

When John Addington Symonds popularized *humanist* and *humanism* in his multivolume *Renaissance in Italy* (1875–1886), he noted in a footnote that the origins of the word *humanist* were "pure Italian," but "the word *Humanism* has a German sound, and is in fact modern." It was indeed first used in Germany during the so-called Enlightenment with a pedagogical meaning, associated with the old ideas of *humanity*, *humanist*, and the *humanities*; and arising around 1800 during the controversy between advocates of old and new systems of education.

The educational reformer Johann Bernhard Basedow founded a model school in 1774 at Dessau in Saxony, based on the ideas of Jean-Jacques Rousseau as expressed in *Emile* (1762), and teaching by doing rather than learning by rote. He described it in the prospectus as "the Philanthropinum, a school of human friendship and good knowledge for pupils and young teachers," and explained:

All men have an inborn drive to human love: (1) Shared feeling for the pain and wretchedness of others; (2) Shared joy for their happiness and their pleasure; (3) Especially friendly love for some individuals.

As a result the first pioneers of modern practical and vocational education called themselves *philanthropinists* and their ideology *philanthropinism*. They called for human feeling to be directed beyond our immediate relations or neighbors or countrymen toward the whole human race. The movement was short-lived, partly because Basedow was hostile to orthodox religion and got into frequent trouble with the authorities and the general public for his open criticisms, and partly because he was a cranky personality and soon left the Philanthropinum, which closed soon afterward

In reaction to the philanthropinists, the defenders of traditional education in Christian religion and classical studies, and also in traditional morality and patriotism, adopted the term *humanism*, echoing *humanist* and *humanities*, and embodying the idea of *Humanität* (humanity) and the ideal of *Bildung* (education and cultivation, but more than either—the equivalent of the Greek *paideia*). The first appearance of the new word in print seems to have been in a book published in 1808 by the Bavarian educationist Friedrich Immanuel Niethammer, *Der Streit des Philanthropinismus und Humanismus in der Theorie des Erziehungs-Unterrichts unsrer Zeit* (The Quarrel of Philanthropinism and Humanism in the Theory of Educational Instruction of Our Time).

Niethammer used the terms *humanism* and *philanthropinism* for the old and new concepts of education, but he extended both concepts beyond the narrowly educational to the wider intellectual arena; thus he broadened the meaning of *humanism* as follows:

The denomination of *humanism* applies not only to the party which defends the study of the so-called *Humaniora* [Humanities] in the academic schools against ill-conceived attacks; it applies in a much more elevated sense to the whole older pedagogy whose basic characteristic was always to care more for the *humanity* than for the *animality* of the pupil, and which continues to voice its claims as a minority opposition against the prevailing modern education for animality.

He acknowledged the value of philanthropinism, whose newfangled ideas had brought necessary reform to the "dead letter" of old-fashioned education, but he attacked it at length and in detail, warning that its materialistic and mechanistic tendencies would lead to what he called *animalism*, not only in schools but in society at large, and that merely practical and utilitarian instruction would destroy the true spirit of cultivation and culture. He condemned the "spiritual revolution" which "in the name of enlightenment" had "degraded religion to common morality, Christianity to eudemonism, theology to naturalism, philosophy to syncretism and materialism, knowledge of the world to knowledge of the earth, and science to sensationalism." But he detected the revival of "a better spirit, the spirit of *humanism*," embodying "the better spirit of *humanity*," which should be manifested in and through the educational system; and he proposed a reformed version of the strongly traditional and frankly elitist curriculum as *humanism*, which in theory combined the best of both old and new methods, but which in practice was still based on the ideas of antiquity, on instruction in Latin and Greek, and also on indoctrination in Christianity.

Hence the influential line that ancient languages and established religion somehow had more to do with *humanness* and *humaneness* and *humanity* and *humanization* than mathematics and science and technology; and hence the traditional sense of *humanism* as education in the *humanities* in schools for the intellectual elite (the *gymnasium* in Germany, the *lycée* in France), as distinct from schools for the technical elite or the mass of the people.

When philanthropinism declined and disappeared, progressive education was developed and publicized by the Swiss reformer Johann Heinrich Pestalozzi. Meanwhile practical as opposed to humanist education was described as *realism*, and there was a long "struggle between *humanism* and *realism*," as described in 1863 by Karl Schmidt in his *Geschichte der Erziehung und des Unterrichts* (History of Education and of Instruction).

Niethammer's line of argument was repeated by later writers. In 1826 the Bavarian educationist Friedrich Thiersch published *Ueber gelehrte Schulen* (On Academic Schools), in which he similarly advocated a combination of the best of both traditions. In 1831 the Württemberg educationist Friedrich Wilhelm Klumpp published *Die gelehrten Schulen nach den Grundsätzen des wahren Humanismus und den Anforderungen der Zeit* (The Academic Schools According to the Principles of True Humanism and the Demands of the Age), in which he attempted to answer "the well-known question of humanism and realism" by combining the best elements of both, and producing what he called a "humanism with a Christian and national tendency" and a "humanism broadened through the sciences." He not only argued his case but put it into practice by opening a school at Stetten which lasted from the 1830s to the 1850s.

And in 1842 the scholar Otto Heinsius entered the controversy with *Konkordat zwischen Schule und Leben, oder Vermittelung des Humanismus und Realismus, aus nationalistischem Standpunkt betrachtet* (Concordat between School and Life, or Mediation of Humanism and Realism, Considered from a Nationalist Position), following a similar line. The review by Max Stirner (Johann Caspar Schmidt) in the *Rheinische Zeitung*, "The False Principle of our Education, or humanism and realism" (April 1842), preferred realism to humanism which inculcated only limited freedom.

Those who adopted *humanism* (*Humanismus*) did so in the sense of the study of the *humanities* (*Humaniora*) rather than of devotion to the idea or concept of *humanity* (*Humanität*), and certainly not with any sentiment of hostility to conventional religion. This was correctly recorded in reference books from H. A. Pierer's *Encyclopädisches Wörterbuch* (1828); but the distinctions could easily be misinterpreted. Thus the Lutheran publicist Karl Kahnis wrote *Der innere Gang des deutschen Protestantismus seit Mitte des vorigen Jahrhunderts* (1854), beginning with a sustained attack on various aspects of the Enlightenment (*Aufklärung*). He misleadingly referred to its ideal normally as *Humanität*, occasionally as *Humanismus*, and seriously distorted its meaning. The admittedly bad English translation by Theodore Meyer, *Internal History of German Protestantism since the Middle of Last Century* (1856), further distorted his argument by eccentric versions of the key words; *Aufklärung* was consistently rendered as *illuminism*, causing confusion with the esoteric Illuminati of Adam Weishaupt, and *Humanität* and *Humanismus* were both rendered as *humanism*, causing confusion between those who did and those who did not use the latter term. Thus Kahnis's argument, in Meyer's version, runs—or stumbles—as follows:

> In the room of the authorities of Church and State, Illuminism [*Aufklärung*] put common sense; in the room of the positive forms of life, a general disposition of mind, becoming man as such, which is termed *Humanism* [*Humanität*]. This Humanism [*Humanität*] levels all family traditions, all differences of rank, all nationality, all positive moral law, all positive religion,—all of them being only accidental numerators for the denominator of mankind: what man wants in the first and last place, that is, to be a *man*. . . .

This was followed by a back-to-front argument that "to a higher form of Humanism [*Humanität*] the classical studies led," which was agreed to be an improvement, though the result was still opposed to religion:

> While Humanism [*Humanismus*] is based on the belief in the excellence of human nature, the Church teaches its utter helplessness for salvation. While Humanism [*Humanismus*] declares the purely human life to be the true life, Christ teaches to flee from the world in order to find life in him. While Humanism [*Humanismus*] is pleased and contented in a bright present, Christianity teaches a pilgrimage to the heavenly Church. . . . Humanism [*Humanismus*] found, neither in the Church nor

in the State, a sphere suitable to it. The State was too material for it, the Church was too spiritual, too superhuman, too much occupied with a future life. . . .

This bore little relation to the actual views of the German educationists who then called themselves humanists, though it bore a striking resemblance to the views of some of the people who later called themselves humanists.

This misleading tale was retold by James Gardner in *The Faiths of the World* (1858–1861), "A Dictionary of All Religions and of Religious Sects, Their Doctrines, Rites, Ceremonies and Customs," published first as a part-work and then in two enormous volumes. The entry on *humanists* began: "A class of thinkers which arose in Germany towards the end of the eighteenth century." But it too identified them with the philanthropinists rather than with their opponents, and commented: "Their views were thoroughly infidel, their chief aim being to sink the *Christian* in the *man*. Hence the name given to their system, which was usually called *Humanism*." And it continued: "The Philanthropic Humanism soon gave place to a higher Humanism, which began to spring out of the ardent study of the ancient classics." This reference unfortunately got into dictionaries, causing unending confusion—though of course both Kahnis (through Meyer) and Gardner uncannily anticipated the later usage of *humanism*.

Historical Humanism

The word *humanism* soon spread beyond the world of education and acquired wider meanings, as *humanist* had done. One was a general quality of humanness, used as early as the 1830s. Another was a specific quality connected with the Italian Renaissance, not so much in the narrow academic sense of the original humanists as in a wider cultural sense altogether.

Edward Gibbon had noted that "the humanists of the fifteenth century had revived the knowledge of the ancients" (*Journal*, February 9, 1764); he took this from Claude Fleury's *Traité du choix et de la méthode des études* (1686), translated as *The History, Choice, and Method of Studies* (1695), which described the "restoration of humanity" (*le renouvellement des humanités*) by "the humanists" (*les humanistes*). This view of the actual practice of the people who were called *humanists* was then projected backward on to a mythical theory of a system which was called *humanism*—a development pioneered by German historians. One of the first publications which named *humanism* as a feature of the age was Karl Hagen's multivolume book of 1841–1843, *Deutschlands literarische und religiöse Verhältnisse im Reformationszeitalter* (Germany's Literary and Religious Relations in the Age of the Reformation); and it was popularized by Georg Voigt's book of 1859, *Die Wiederbelebung des classischen Althertums, oder das erste Jahrhundert des Humanismus* (The Revival of Classical Antiquity, or the First Century of Humanism).

Jacob Burckhardt's book of 1860, *Die Cultur der Renaissance in Italien* (The Civilization of the Renaissance in Italy), repeated this use of *humanism*, and also popularized the sense of *Renaissance*. This derived from the use in 1550 by Giorgio Vasari in his *Vite de' più eccellenti pittori, scultori ed architetti* (Lives of the Most Excellent Painters, Sculptors and Architects) of the term *rinascita* (rebirth) to mean the revival of classical art, and it was now extended to cover the revival of classical languages and literature, philosophy and politics, and culture in general.

When J. A. Symonds popularized this idea in English, he offered an unmistakably ideological definition of *humanism* "in the widest sense of the word" in the second volume of his *Renaissance in Italy* (1877):

> The essence of humanism consisted in a new and vital perception of the
> dignity of man as a rational being apart from theological determina-

tions, and in the further perception that classical literature alone displayed human nature in the plenitude of intellectual and moral freedom. It was partly a reaction against ecclesiastical despotism, partly an attempt to find the point of unity for all that had been thought and done by man, within the mind restored to consciousness of its own faculty.

Thus *humanism* during the nineteenth century was applied retrospectively and indeed anachronistically and unhistorically to the fifteenth century, and critical controversy between Scholastic and humanist scholarship was reinterpreted as doctrinal controversy between theistic and humanistic belief. Specialist historians attempted to restrict the term to the area of classical scholarship in Italy or of classical education in Germany, but most historians tended to expand it, and the common historical meaning of *humanism* in all languages became not just scholarship or instruction in classical studies but the concentration on the human individual and personality, the human mind and body, human worth and welfare, human power and progress, human freedom and fate, humanity in general, which was considered to be characteristic of the Renaissance, in Italy and then elsewhere in Europe. A much-needed but little-heeded deflation of this myth appeared in the introduction to C. S. Lewis's *English Literature in the Sixteenth Century* (1954).

This process of widening definition led to the description as humanists of many people who were not really humanists in the original strict sense—such as Francesco Petrarca (the fourteenth-century poet Petrarch, Voigt's hero, who was indeed a pioneer of classical studies, though not an academic), Giovanni Boccaccio and Geoffrey Chaucer, Giovanni Pico della Mirandola and Marsilio Ficino, Leonardo da Vinci and Michelangelo Buonarroti, Leon Battista Alberti and Juan Luis Vives, Niccolò Machiavelli and Francesco Guicciardini, Desiderius Erasmus and Thomas More, François Rabelais and Michel de Montaigne, Johannes Reuchlin and Ulrich von Hutten.

This sense was later qualified as *Renaissance humanism*, and then

extended both backward and forward in history. The ideas of antiquity
and of the Middle Ages which had foreshadowed Renaissance humanism were called *classical humanism* and *medieval humanism* respectively, and the ideas of the early modern world which followed
Renaissance humanism in differing ways have been variously called
Enlightenment humanism (for France), *new humanism* or *third humanism* (for Germany), and *Augustan humanism* (for Britain). The term
was also extended sideways. The specifically political ideas which
were considered to be especially characteristic of the Renaissance, as
expressed by Machiavelli and Guicciardini, were called *civic humanism*. The intellectual ideas of the Italian Renaissance which had particular appeal north of the Alps, as expressed by Erasmus and More,
were called *northern humanism*. Later there were such varieties as
juridic humanism for scholars of Roman law.

Like *humanist*, *humanism* acquired vaguer meanings—equivalent
to humanness or humanitarianism, human rather than divine interests,
academic rather than technical education, aesthetic or emotional rather
than scientific or rational attitudes—and was often employed with
little or no meaning at all. Thus R. B. Haldane's book *The Philosophy
of Humanism* (1922)—which actually said virtually nothing about
humanism in any sense—defined it as "what conforms to the standards
of value in domains such as those of Literature, of Music, of Art, and
of Religion," as distinct from mathematics and science—the values of
the humanities.

Humanisms in the Nineteenth Century

The word *humanism* was increasingly used during the nineteenth century by many very different people and acquired several new meanings in addition to the old ones.

English Unitarianism

The earliest appearance of *humanism* in English seems to be in a collection called *Omniana*, written in 1812 and first published in the first volume of *The Literary Remains of Samuel Taylor Coleridge* (1836). This contains an essay on "Religion" which includes a criticism of the heresy of Socinianism, with the remark that a Socinian is "a man who has passed from orthodoxy to the loosest Arminianism, and thence to Arianism, and thence to direct Humanism," and is likely "to fall off into the hopeless abyss of atheism."

Coleridge was using the word *humanism* in the sense of *Unitari-*

anism, the doctrine that God has only one person and that Jesus was only human. (William Wilberforce, the Evangelical Christian politician and reformer, similarly described Unitarianism as "a sort of halfway house . . . a stage on the journey" from orthodoxy to infidelity.) Unitarians didn't themselves use the word then, but some did so later, and eventually American Unitarians played a crucial part in altering its meaning.

Philosophical Humanism

Another precise sense was developed in Germany later in the early nineteenth century. Some of the philosophers who followed G. W. F. Hegel—or rather, transcended or negated him—and were called "Young Hegelians," developed a radical critique of religion, turning it upside down, arguing that it had put God in the place of man and that philosophy should put man in the place of God. Eventually this movement adopted the word *humanism*, a tendency led by Arnold Ruge, the main editor of successive magazines of the Young Hegelians. For example, when he reviewed Heinrich Christoph von Gagern's *Critik des Völkerrechts, mit practischer Anwendung auf unsre Zeit* (Critique of International Law, with Practical Application to Our Time) in the *Hallische Jahrbücher* (June 24–30, 1840), he referred several times to the author's *humanism*, meaning his adoption of the philosophical idea of humanity rather than the educational theory of the humanities. Such cultural usage was acceptable, but parallel religious usage was not. When Ruge discussed "The Restoration of Christianity" in the *Deutsche Jahrbücher* (December 27–29, 1841), the censors suppressed a sensitive sentence which was restored when the essay was reprinted in the third volume of his *Gesammelte Schriften* (Collected Writings) in 1846: "The old form of religion is Christian belief, or *old* Christianity; the new religion is *realized* Christianity, or *humanism*."

The influential publications of David Friedrich Strauss, which insisted on a naturalistic interpretation of the Gospel stories and contrasted the "Old Faith" with the "New Faith," and of the Feuerbach brothers, which insisted on the replacement of God by man, prepared the ground for the spread of this use of the term *humanism*. Ludwig Feuerbach said in *The Essence of Christianity* (1841) that man had made God in his own image, but that man was the Supreme Being to man, and that theology should be replaced by what he called *anthropology*; Friedrich Feuerbach said in *The Religion of the Future* (1843–1845) that religion should be based on man rather than God, that the supreme quality was not divinity but humanity.

Neither Strauss nor the Feuerbachs used the word *humanism* in their published work—though Ludwig Feuerbach did say in one of his manuscript fragments (posthumously published by Karl Grün in 1874) that if anyone wanted foreign words for his system they could use "humanism or anthropologism." Commentators soon adopted the former. One who wrote as "an Epigone" produced a book in 1852 on *Die Triarier: David Friedrich Strauss, Ludwig Feuerbach und Arnold Ruge, und ihr Kampf für die moderne Geistesfreiheit* (The Triarii [veteran soldiers]: David Friedrich Strauss, Ludwig Feuerbach and Arnold Ruge, and Their Struggle for Modern Intellectual Freedom), describing Feuerbach as "one of the genial prophets of humanism, that is the humane, purely human religion of the future," and describing Ruge as "the practitioner of humanism," "who filled his heart and soul with the idea of humanism."

Various other new words were proposed as well. Friedrich Feuerbach used *Theanthropos* as a pseudonym in 1838 for his book *Eine Reihe von Aphorismen* (A Series of Aphorisms), and Ludwig Feuerbach half-seriously suggested both *theoanthropism* and *anthropotheism* in letters in 1842. But when Ruge went into exile in France in 1843, he popularized the new sense of the old word *humanism*, arguing in a letter to a friend for "humanism as principle and system" (November 23, 1844) and equating it with the French "*principe humanitaire*." Here the word began to acquire a meaning similar to the one we use, in which religion is replaced by philosophy, magic by science, God by man, divinity by humanity—and theism by humanism.

In 1844 Ruge and Karl Marx produced a single issue of a new magazine, *Deutsch-Französische Jahrbücher* (in which appeared Marx's infamous description of religion as "the *opium* of the people"). A section publishing correspondence dating from 1843 included several examples of the new use of *humanism*. The Russian revolutionary Michael Bakunin (whose essay on "The Reaction in Germany"—with its infamous peroration, "The urge for destruction is also a creative urge!"—had appeared in the *Deutsche Jahrbücher* in October 1842) wrote in May 1843:

> A great enthusiasm for humanism and for the state, whose principle is now finally truly man, a burning hatred of priests and their impudent defilement of all that is humanly great and true, again fills the world.

Bakunin later turned against the state, becoming the main founder of the anarchist movement; and in 1871 he wrote in *God and the State* (1882) that "if God really existed, he would have to be abolished."

Ruge's introductory "Plan" for the *Deutsch-Französische Jahrbücher* emphasized the significance of the French revolutionary tradition and explained the spirit which inspired the project:

> France is the political principle, the pure principle of human freedom in Europe and France is alone in this. It has proclaimed and conquered human rights, it has lost and regained its conquest, it struggles at this instant for the realization of the great principles of humanism, which the Revolution brought into the world. . . . The real unification of the German and French spirit is a coming together in the principle of humanism. . . .

In 1845 he published *Unsre letzten zehn Jahre: Ueber die neuste deutsche Philosophie* (Our Last Ten Years: On the Latest German Philosophy), in which he frequently used the word *humanism* in this sense. He identified Feuerbach's philosophy as such, with the comment:

The explanation of religion (and Christianity is the highest form of religion) from the essence of man—*theoretical humanism*—and the constitution of human society deduced from the claim of all individuals to real human existence—*practical humanism*—finally the unification of both sides: the true cult, which is none other than the true culture of man and his world—the solutions of the great problem of history. . . .

He identified the socialism of the *Deutsch-Französische Jahrbücher* as "practical humanism, the humanism of common life," with the comment:

It is obvious that the emancipation of the civilized and the enlightenment of religious man have in *humanism* their common principle and in happiness of the most real human existence their common aim.

However, he refused to follow Etienne Cabet or Karl Marx and adopt communism, commenting in a letter to his wife Agnes that "the communists are not humanists, except that they seek to make men into men, which is humanism" (August 11, 1843).

Ruge's philosophical humanism applied to both politics and religion. His essay on "Patriotism," included in the sixth volume of his *Gesammelte Schriften* (1847), advocated "the transcendence of patriotism in humanism" and argued that "the theories of humanism are now already working against religious and patriotic fanaticism." His "Philosophical Pocketbook," *Die Akademie* (1848), included an article on "The Religion of Our Time," which discussed Jewish, Greek, Roman, and Christian religion, and ended by describing "the struggle for humanism"—a "human religion," which would be "a transcendence of religion."

When he settled in permanent exile in Britain in 1848, after the failure of revolution and the triumph of reaction in both Germany and France, he introduced the new sense of *humanism* into English. In August 1850 he sent a message (in English) to the Frankfurt Peace Congress, "Let the philosophical humanism join the religious humanism!" adding that "the one great cause . . . is the realization of humanity and Christianity." During 1852–1853 he gave lectures (in English) which were published in Holyoake's Cabinet of Reason series as *The New Germany* (1854).

Ruge explained in the introduction that his lectures "might be considered as a CATECHISM OF HUMANISM for freethinking men," and proclaimed that "the religion of our time is Humanism." In the second section he expounded what he called "The Lodge of Humanism." He argued that religion went through several stages—the worship of fetishes, of nature, of the universe, of beauty, of virtue, of creation—culminating in Christianity, which apparently worships God as man but actually worships man as God. The Trinity really expressed not three persons of the deity but three aspects of humanity, and it was time to go on to the next stage: "As soon as this meaning of Christianism is discovered, the whole Christian heaven falls to the earth, and a new religion is originated, the religion of Humanism."

"Our task," Ruge told his mainly German audience, was "*to create, in the midst of tyranny, the Lodge of Humanism, the invisible church of humanity, voluntary freemasonry for our principles, an open conspiracy for the safety of all the achievements of the German genius; and to foster the belief in the unity and Liberty of our nation, the savior of all the rest*" (original emphasis). He advocated the combination of classical and Renaissance ideals with the literary work of Goethe and Schiller and the philosophical work of Herder and Hegel into what he called "real Humanism." He added that "real Humanism has to abolish neither philosophy nor religion, but to establish a new system of both, or to realize the German philosophy and the Christian religion," and explained that "the real religious activity is to raise every man to his human reality, in a political and commercial community of equal associates." He invoked the example of radical Christians as well as revolutionary politicians.

He continued that "Humanism is the combination of the scientific and popular system of our time," that "Humanism pretends [claims] to make every individual a free man, free in intellectual, aesthetical, and moral or social respects," and that "the religion of Humanism intends to realize the idea of humanity by knowledge, beauty, and liberty."

> Real freedom will exist when the contradictions between freethought and enslaved mankind are dissolved. Freethinking men make the unconscious self-determination of their history a self-conscious one. Only the free man is a real human being—the realizing of the theoretical freedom is free humanity. Such *humanizing of the world* we call *Humanism.*

To this end he advocated "the establishing of the *communities, schools* and *academies of Humanism,*" which would work for a "democratic republic" combining liberalism and socialism, or individualism and communism.

According to the autobiographical *Past and Thoughts* of his Russian fellow exile Alexander Herzen, Ruge's lectures were badly presented and badly attended, and his *humanism* doesn't seem to have had much impact outside or even inside the German community. Nevertheless, although Ruge failed to found a humanist movement at the time, he anticipated many of the ideas of what was called the humanist movement a century later.

There were similar and simultaneous developments among German exiles who came from a religious rather than a political background. During the late 1840s, several groups of former Catholics and Protestants formed Free Religious Congregations (*Freie Religiösen Gemeinden*) in parts of Germany and Austria, and after 1848 some of their members settled in Britain and the United States. They often included *humanity* among their ideals and described their new faith as the *religion of humanity,* and sometimes called themselves *humanists* and called their ideology *humanism.* In Britain, for example, when Carl Scholl described "The New Reform in Germany" in Holyoake's paper *The Reasoner* (March 5–May 21, 1851) he insisted that it was "no obstacle to the purposes of Socialism, Democracy, Humanism"; and when Johannes Ronge (the main founder of the German Catholic Church in 1845) described *The Reformation of the Nineteenth Century*

(1852), he included among its aims "the principles of humanism." Ronge later founded a Humanistic Association, which held public meetings in London in 1854–1856 and advocated what John Ellis, one of its members, called "the religion of humanism" (*The Reasoner*, December 17, 1854). This religious movement was as transient as Ruge's political program in Britain, though it foreshadowed the Positivist movement which began a few years later, it lasted longer in the United States, and it flourished in Germany for more than a century. (Ronge's more permanent contribution to British life was by joining his wife Bertha Ronge in introducing Friedrich Froebel's kindergarten system of infant education.)

Political Humanism

The concept of philosophical *humanism* attracted religious and right-wing criticism, of course, but also nonreligious and left-wing criticism.

Thus Karl Marx and Friedrich Engels, who began as Young Hegelians but soon established their own tradition, approved of *humanism* for getting away from religion, but disapproved of it for not going far enough toward revolution. Marx's first major composition, the so-called *Economic and Philosophical Manuscripts* (written in 1844, but not published until 1932), included striking passages on the subject:

> Communism as fully developed naturalism equals humanism, and as fully developed humanism equals naturalism; it is the *genuine* resolution of the conflict between man and nature and man and man. . . . Atheism as the transcendence of God is the emergence of theoretical humanism, and communism as the transcendence of private property is the vindication of real human life as man's property—the emergence of practical humanism. Atheism is humanism mediated through itself by the transcendence of religion, and communism is humanism mediated through itself by the transcendence of private property. Only through the transcendence of this mediation . . . does positively self-deriving humanism, *positive* humanism, come into being.

Marx and Engels began their first published book, *The Holy Family* (1845), by defending their "real humanism" against the abstract versions of other writers (just as they later defended their "scientific socialism" against the "utopian socialism" of other writers); and they spent much of *The German Ideology* (written in 1845–1846, but not published until 1903–1932) criticizing other writers' versions of humanism. They quickly dropped the term, but their followers subsequently picked it up again.

In 1845 one of their main targets, Max Stirner, who had previously criticized educational humanism, spent much of his masterpiece *Der Einzige und sein Eigenthum* (The Ego and His Own) also welcoming the denial of divinity but criticizing the worship of humanity; he didn't call this *humanism*, but Ruge described his book as a "Critique of Liberalism, Socialism and Humanism."

Another of Marx's targets, the French socialist Pierre Joseph Proudhon (who in 1840 made the scandalous statement, "Property is theft" and was the first person to call himself an anarchist), similarly agreed with the atheism of the Left Hegelians, but disagreed with their humanism. When he was introduced by Karl Grün to French translations of the Feuerbach brothers, in 1844–1845, he made hostile marginal comments: "I can be neither spiritualist, nor materialist, nor atheist, nor humanist. . . . I reject all mysticisms. . . . Humanism is a false religion." He elaborated this in his next book, *System of Economic Contradictions: or, Philosophy of Poverty* (1846). His major assault on religion—culminating in the scandalous statement, "God is evil"—included a minor attack on "the *humanists*, the new atheists":

As for me, I regret to say, for I feel that such a declaration separates me from the most intelligent party of socialism, it is impossible for me, the more I think about it, to subscribe to this deification of our species, which is at bottom among the new atheists, only a last echo of religious terrors; who under the name of *humanism*, rehabilitating and consecrating mysticism, restore prejudice back to science, custom back to morality, community, that is atony and poverty, back to social economy, absurdity back

> to logic. It is impossible for me, I say, to accept this new religion, in which
> they vainly try to interest me by telling me that I am its god.

He accused the humanists of simply replacing God by man:

> God, according to the humanists, is nothing but humanity itself, the col-
> lective me to which the individual me is subjected as to an invisible master.
> . . . It is no longer man; it is God. Humanism is the most perfect theism.

He argued that "humanism is a religion as detestable as any of the
theisms of ancient origin," and that it was necessary to "reject humanism" because it "tended invincibly, by the deification of humanity,
to a religious restoration." Yet, he insisted, "I do not contradict
humanism; I continue it"; and he insisted on "the necessity of atheism
for the physical, moral and intellectual perfecting of man." What he
objected to was the religious flavor of German humanism; and he took
the same view of French attempts to replace orthodox religion with a
new "Religion of Humanity."

Religions of Humanity

In France, indeed, philosophical humanism turned in a much more
overtly religious direction.

Many attempts had been made to form or re-form a religion based on
reason, nature, and science. During the eighteenth century the deists
called for natural religion, and the Freemasons developed an esoteric version of one—expressed openly in 1791 in W. A. Mozart's last opera, *Die
Zauberflöte* (The Magic Flute), whose libretto by Emanuel Schikaneder
repeatedly invokes humanity. In 1762 Rousseau in *Du contrat social* (On
the Social Contract) called for a deistic "civil religion" to support his ideal
state, based on "sentiments of sociability" rather than "religious dogmas."

During the French Revolution, several new "natural" and "social"
religions were proposed; in 1793 Festivals of Reason were celebrated,

and in 1794 an official Cult of the Supreme Being was proclaimed. In 1796 Jean-Baptiste Chemin-Dupontès proposed the formation of a "Society of Theoanthropophiles"; and in 1797 he and Valentin Haüy formed a "Society of Theophilanthropes," of which Thomas Paine was an active member. As *theophilanthropists*, or "Adorers of God and Friends of Men," this deistic and humanistic sect prospered under the Directory, especially through the patronage of one of its members, Louis-Marie La Réveillière-Lépeaux; but when Napoléon took power and made a Concordat with the Vatican he suppressed them in 1801. (Theophilanthropists survived underground for a time, were absorbed into the Freemasons, and revived briefly in the 1880s.)

Later the French socialist Henri de Saint-Simon called in a pamphlet for a *New Christianity* (1825), rejecting all existing forms, based on the rule, "All men ought to act towards each other as brothers," and led by scientists, artists and industrialists. The French socialist Etienne Cabet called in his utopian novel *Voyage to Icaria* (1840), and also in his later actual colonies, for a "religion of community." He named the ideal of his communism as "humanity"; again Ruge called it *humanism*.

The French socialist Pierre Leroux had appealed for a new "Religion of Humanity" in his book *De l'égalité* (1838), and he explained it at enormous length in his book *De l'humanité* (1840)—"On Humanity, on its Principle, and on its Future, where is expounded the True Definition of Religion, and where is explained the Direction, the Result, and the Connection of Mosaism and Christianity." But the idea of Leroux was generally called *humanitaire* rather than *humaniste*. There was room for confusion here as well, since what was called *humanitarisme* in the short-lived group and magazine both inspired by Gabriel Charavay and both called *L'Humanitaire* (1841), which became the subject of a sedition trial, combined atheist materialism with libertarian communism and rejected religion.

The French social scientist Auguste Comte (the founder of sociology in 1824), who was a colleague and then an opponent of Saint-Simon and a rival of Leroux, followed a similar line but went much further. His enormously ambitious "Positive Philosophy," with its tripartite view of human history with three "states" ("theological state, or fictive; metaphysical state, or abstract; scientific state, or positive"), was eventually extended from its original social and political mission ("Love for principle; order for basis; progress for end") in an increasingly religious direction ("Live for others").

The "General Conclusion of the Preliminary Discourse" (1848) in the first volume of his final *Système de Politique Positive* (1851) expounded his version of the "Religion of Humanity"—deity replaced by humanity, seen as "the Great Being" and the "new Supreme Being," with Comte himself the "High Priest of Humanity," worship of God replaced by worship of man, represented by particular great men and women or by the general spirit of the species, with elaborate ritual in formal services. Later Positivist doctrine and worship were respectively dismissed by T. H. Huxley as "Catholicism minus Christianity" and by Mark Pattison as "three persons and no God"; but the movement founded by Comte did have a partial and temporary success in France and also in other countries, including Britain (and especially Brazil, where there is still an active Positivist movement).

The followers of Comte were generally described as *Positivists* rather than *humanists*, but in English the word *humanism* was sometimes applied to their ideology, especially by outsiders. Thus W. E. Gladstone referred in an account of unorthodox ideas about religion to "Positivism or Comtism, or, as it might be called, Humanism" (*Contemporary Review*, June 1876). W. K. Clifford remarked in a symposium on "The Influence upon Morality of a Decline in Religious Belief" (*Nineteenth Century*, April 1877):

I neither admit the moral influence of theism in the past, nor look forward to the moral influence of humanism in the future.

This was moving beyond positivism to a more general view of humanism. Alfred Barratt went further in his posthumous *Physical Metempiric* (1883), expounding his evolutionary view of ethics:

> The higher good is thus gradually raised above the lower; Altruism (for instance) or Utilitarianism, which is the conservation of societies, the end of Politics, overshadows the Egoism on which rests the morality of individual men, and already shows occasional symptoms of fading into a higher Humanism.

The American writer Edward H. Griggs also advocated "The Religion of Humanity" in *The New Humanism* (1900), but this was not so much a true religion as a vague idealism combining classical and Christian ideas.

British Secularism

British freethinkers seldom mentioned *humanism* during the nineteenth century. Their main leader, G. J. Holyoake, who began by following the rational religion or rationalism of Robert Owen—as in *Rationalism: A Treatise for the Times* (1845)—later advocated naturalism, realism, and cosmism, but in 1851 he adopted the new term *secularism*, rejecting both theism and atheism, avoiding theoretical discussions of ultimate questions, and concentrating on the practical issues of this life in this world. His many defences of secularism identified it mainly with the Positivism of Comte. In *Secularism, the Philosophy of the People* (1854), he based it on "humanity" without mentioning humanism; but in *The Principles of Secularism Briefly Explained* (1859) he gave a more detailed "Definition of Principles":

> The leading ideas of Secularism are Humanism, Moralism, Materialism, Utilitarian unity: humanism the physical perfection of this life—moralism founded on the laws of Nature, as the guidance of this life—materialism as the means of Nature for the Secular improvement of this life—unity upon this three-fold ground of Positivism.

He occasionally returned to the word. In a lecture published as *The Limits of Atheism* (1861), he discussed various forms of atheism. He opposed "Negative Atheism" with "Affirmative Atheism," which he identified with secularism and cosmism, and whose principles he listed as "Positivism in Principle, Exactness in Profession of Opinion, Dispassionateness in Judgment, Humanism in Conception"—the latter meaning "Reliance upon Humanity." But he didn't follow up such hints in the rest of his long career, and later returned to *rationalism* (becoming the first chairman of the Rationalist Press Association in 1899).

A Scottish freethinker who wrote as "A. C." discussed various terms in a series of autobiographical articles on his "Theological Experience: A Journey from Christianity to Freethought" (*National Reformer*, April 8–29, 1866). He said of the freethinkers:

> They have broken up the soil with the plough of ridicule—laid out the grounds upon the plans of Rationalism, projected the arbors of Socialism, remodelled their projects under the name of Secularism, and schemed or favored other isms—as Eclecticism, Positivism, Humanism, Cosmism. . . .

And he ended by preferring the old word *Christianity* to "any of the new ones which have been coined":

> Socialism conveys an idea of jollity and good living. Secularism conveys an idea of material economy, but none of a governing sentiment. Humanism suggests frailty and crime as well as virtue and rectitude; they are all alike human. . . .

These were common objections. Charles Bradlaugh, Holyoake's main rival and then successor, who founded the National Secular Society in 1866, doesn't seem to have used the word at all. Neither did his American counterpart, Robert G. Ingersoll (though he said that "humanity is the grand religion" and referred to the "great gospel of humanity"). And Bradlaugh's successors G. W. Foote and Chapman Cohen used it only in the general historical and cultural sense.

Humanitarianism and Other Humanisms

The word *humanitarianism* was used in most of the noncultural meanings of *humanism*, in English as in French, but it was eventually narrowed from the general sense of humaneness to mean particular attention to the suffering of human victims or animals, as used by Humanitarian Leagues in several countries and in the British paper called *Humanity* and then the *Humanitarian* (1892–1919). But it could still be used to mean something closer to *humanism*, as in the *Humanitarian Review* published in Los Angeles from 1903 to 1911, which included among its interests "scientific rationalism," "ethical culture," and "freethought." And *humanitarianism* was sometimes equated with *secularism*, even by Bradlaugh (*National Reformer*, August 24, 1861), and later by several other people, especially Joachim Kaspary during the 1870s and 1880s.

An independent version of *humanism* was expounded in 1858 by the Danish philosopher Gabriel Sibbern in *Om Humanisme* (On Humanism). This proposed an abstract concept of humanism, seen as a "view of life" (*livsanskuelse*) depending on reason, opposed to an abstract concept of positivism depending on revelation. It seems to have had little or no impact.

The German philosopher Friedrich Nietzsche was no kind of humanist, because of his low view of humanity as it is; he condemned not just man (*Mensch*) but also various forms of man—"Common Man," "Good Man," "Modern Man," "Future Man," "Subman," even "Unman." But because of his high view of humanity as it might be, he was sometimes called a *superhumanist* or *ultrahumanist*. "I teach you the Superman" (or "Overman": *Übermensch*), he wrote in 1883 in his best-known book *Also sprach Zarathustra* (Thus Spake Zoroaster); "Man is something that should be surpassed" (or "overcome": *überwunden*). He took the concept of the Superman from ancient Greece—*huperanthropos* appears in the writings of Dionysius of Halicarnassus and Lucian—and he anticipated some of the concepts of so-called *transhumanism* and *posthumanism* independently suggested by several people a century later.

The life-centered and action-centered ethics of the French moral philosopher Jean Marie Guyau and the German moral philosopher Rudolf Eucken were both occasionally called *humanism* by others, though not by either of them.

Women seem to have played little or no part in the various manifestations of humanism so far described, though *woman* had a very exalted place in Comte's religion of humanity. But humanism did appear in the feminist movement at the end of the nineteenth century. In 1897 Léopold Lacour, a leading French feminist, published a book called *Humanisme intégral* (Integral Humanism), dedicated "To the Apostles, Men and Women, of the Religion of Humanity, of Integral Humanism," which called for feminism to be extended to cover the complete equality of the sexes in a "Humanism no longer Virilist, but Integral," and which identified "true Feminism" with "Integral Humanism." And Laurence Housman, a leading British feminist, later published a pamphlet called *The New Humanism* (1923), which stated that "the New Humanism" would come when the sex-war was succeeded by the sex-peace, and that "the Woman's Movement" was "but a symptomatic part of the whole Humanist movement."

It may be said that by the end of the nineteenth century our sense of humanism had been planted but hadn't quite taken root.

Humanisms in the Twentieth Century

The word *humanism* was claimed by more quite separate groups during the twentieth century, until it was adopted by what became the humanist movement.

Pragmatism

The first deliberate and permanent adoption of *humanism* by a particular intellectual system appeared in the philosophical doctrine of Pragmatism, which was initiated in the United States during the late nineteenth century by C. S. Peirce and William James. *Pragmatism* may be defined as the theory that the truth of a proposition depends not on its correspondence to abstract reality but on its effects in human practice—what is "true" is what "works." It was popular in a country where and in an age when man was able to work and to make things work more effectively than ever before.

Pragmatism soon spread beyond the United States, and its main British exponent, F. C. S. Schiller, who taught at Oxford University from 1897 to 1926, preferred to call it *humanism*—as in his books *Humanism* (1903) and *Studies in Humanism* (1907). In the preface to the former he explained that Pragmatism is based on the saying of Protagoras, and he continued:

> I propose, accordingly, to convert to the use of philosophic terminology a word which has long been found in history and literature, and to denominate HUMANISM the attitude of thought which I know to be habitual in William James and myself, which seems to be sporadic and inchoate in many others, and which is destined, I believe, to win the widest popularity. . . .
>
> Humanism, like Common Sense, of which it may fairly claim to be the philosophic working out, takes Man for granted as he stands, and the world of man's experience as it has come to seem to him. . . .
>
> Humanism is fully able to vindicate itself, and so we can now define it as the philosophic attitude which, without wasting thought upon attempts to construct experience *a priori*, is content to take human experience as the clue to the world of human experience, content to take Man on his own merits, just as he is to start with, without insisting that he must first be disembowelled of his interests and have his individuality evaporated and translated into technical jargon, before he can be deemed deserving of scientific notice. To remember that Man is the measure of all things, *i.e.* of his whole experience-world, and that if our standard measure be proved false all our measurements are vitiated; to remember that Man is the maker of the sciences which subserve his human purposes; to remember that an ultimate philosophy which analyses us away is thereby merely exhibiting its failure to achieve its purpose, that, and more that might be stated to the same effect, is the real root of Humanism.

In "Pragmatism and Humanism," included in *Studies in Humanism*, he defined humanism as "merely the perception that the philosophic problem concerns human beings striving to comprehend a world of human experience by the resources of human minds." And in his contribution to the first series of *Contemporary British Philos-*

ophy: Personal Statements (1924), he answered the question "Why Humanism?" by saying that it was adopted as "the systematic protest against the artificial elimination of the human aspects of knowing in the intellectualist versions of logic and psychology," and that he saw it "as an attitude of the human spirit and as a method of solving the problems of human knowing, rather than as a metaphysical doctrine about reality as such."

He proposed that humanism should supersede both rationalism and empiricism and oppose both supernaturalism and naturalism, explaining in "The Humanistic View of Life" (1935), published in the posthumous collection *Our Human Truths* (1939), that "we may call the attitude of submission to the course of nature that of *naturalism*, while that of striving for the control of nature may be denominated *humanism*." It should also oppose absolutism, as well as both barbarism and Scholasticism. He optimistically alleged that the humanist "will tend to grow *humane*, and tolerant of the divergences of attitude which must inevitably spring from the divergent idiosyncrasies of men." But in *Tantalus, or the Future of Man* (1924), he pessimistically acknowledged: "There is little doubt that, in the main, humanity is still Yahoo-manity." His humanism went only so far.

Schiller had admitted in the preface to *Humanism* that "a complete statement of the Humanist position far transcends, not only my own powers, but those of any single man," but he concluded:

> I thought the good ship Humanism might sail on its adventurous quest for the Islands of the Blest with the lighter freight of these essays as safely and hopefully as with the heaviest cargo.

William James agreed in his essay "Humanism and Truth" (1904), in *The Meaning of Truth* (1909), that what he called "the wider Pragmatism"—the less technical sense—should indeed be called *humanism*, though he added in "Humanism" (1904), reprinted in *Collected Essays and Reviews* (1920), that "*Humanism* is perhaps too 'wholehearted' for the use of philosophers."

The obvious objection was made by the German neo-Kantian philosopher Wilhelm Windelband, who said in his *Introduction to Philosophy* (1914): "Pragmatism is also called *Humanism*—though, in order to avoid confusion with an older and better use of the term, it would be advisable to say *Hominism.*"

Hominism was also used in various similar senses by other German thinkers, such as Friedrich Mauthner and Werner Sombart.

Humanism in Schiller's particular sense didn't long survive Schiller himself, even in Britain, partly because he claimed almost proprietary rights over the word. It was occasionally used by other Pragmatists and also by some other American philosophers, such as George Santayana and John Dewey, though they both preferred other terms. Santayana did occasionally accept the description, but he called humanism "an accomplishment, not a doctrine," and mischievously added in his autobiographical *Apologia pro mente sua* (1940), "My humanism was entirely confined to man."

The word was also used by social scientists like James Leuba and Lewis Mumford, and by publicists like Clarence Darrow and H. L. Mencken. Walter Lippmann's influential book *A Preface to Morals* (1929) proposed a new morality, *humanism*, "centered not in superhuman but in human nature." A section on "The Foundations of Humanism" explained that "when men can no longer be theists, they must, if they are civilized, become humanists," and admitted that "a morality of humanism presents far greater difficulties than a morality premised on theism." The rest of the book consisted of an impressive outline of such a morality.

All these senses of *humanism* were opposed by orthodox thinkers. A. J. Balfour often wrote in favor of theism and against naturalism, including the Gifford Lectures of 1914, *Theism and Humanism* (1915); though in fact he said little about the latter except that "Humanism without Theism loses more than half its value." And G. K. Chesterton protested: "I do not believe that humanism can be a complete substitute for superhumanism."

Cultural Humanism

During the early twentieth century there were occasional revivals of earlier meanings. The American literary critics Irving Babbitt and Paul Elmer More used *humanism* or *new humanism* to describe their traditionalist and elitist view of culture, which became the subject of considerable controversy. Their views were expressed in Norman Foerster's symposium *Humanism and America* (1930), and those of their opponents in C. H. Grattan's symposium *The Critique of Humanism* (1930). Babbitt began his book *Democracy and Leadership* (1924) with a chapter "What Is Humanism?" and contributed to *Humanism and America* "Humanism: An Essay at Definition"—though he actually provided neither a clear answer nor a clear definition. He rejected religion, but other literary humanists did not.

The English writers T. E. Hulme—in his *Speculations: Essays on Humanism and the Philosophy of Art* (1924)—and Percy Wyndham Lewis criticized humanism for its tendencies to "slop" and "slush." The Anglo-American writer T. S. Eliot took a more ambiguous line. He called himself a humanist in the cultural sense, but disliked what he called *paganism* and *skepticism*, and dismissed humanism in the philosophical sense by denying the possibility of its existence as a genuine phenomenon. In a critique of "The Humanism of Irving Babbitt" (1928), he noted that humanism was described as an "*alternative* to religion," and asked:

> Is this alternative any more than a *substitute*? . . . Is it, in the end, a view of life that will work by itself, or is it a derivative of religion which will work only for a short time in history? . . . Is it, in other words, durable beyond one or two generations?

He answered:

> There is no humanistic habit: humanism is, I think, merely the state of mind of a few persons in a few places at a few times. . . . Humanism is either an

> alternative to religion, or is ancillary to it. . . . The humanistic point of view is auxiliary to and dependent upon the religious point of view.

And he returned to the attack in "Second Thoughts on Humanism" (1929); both included in *Selected Essays* (1932).

Lawrence Hyde criticized "modern Humanism" in contemporary literature in *The Prospects of Humanism* (1931), and Colin Wilson criticized "Rational Humanism" in *The Outsider* (1956), though neither had a clear view of their target; Colin Wilson later moved toward religious humanism in *Beyond the Outsider* (1965), but his explanation of it remained unclear (*Humanist*, April 1965). On the other hand, the English critic F. R. Leavis tried to rehabilitate humanism in a nonreligious and anti-utilitarian sense, opposing it to scientism or materialism, and replacing the study of Greek and Latin with that of English.

The broader cultural meaning of *humanism* became increasingly popular in an age when human values were threatened by both religious and nonreligious dogmatism on both right and left. There were international conferences of European intellectuals before and after the Second World War which called for a "new humanism" in the face first of rival totalitarian dictatorships and then of rival nuclear powers. The German novelists Thomas Mann and Heinrich Mann, who were brothers but political opponents, both used *humanism* to describe their positions in opposition to the rival forms of totalitarianism struggling in Germany. In 1924 one of the themes of Thomas Mann's philosophical novel *Der Zauberberg* (The Magic Mountain) was a confrontation between dogmatic humanism (represented by a fanatical Freemason) and dogmatic Christianity (represented by a fanatical Jesuit) and the rejection of both in favor of mere humanity.

Humanism was adopted by or applied to such diverse figures as Alain (Emile Chartier), Isaac Asimov, Margaret Atwood, Arnold Bennett, Bjørnstjerne Bjørnson, Edward Bond, Albert Camus, Karel Capek, Paul Eluard (Eugène Grindel), E. M. Forster, Anatole France (Anatole Thibault), John Galsworthy, André Gide, Maxim Gorky

(Alexei Peshkov), Sinclair Lewis, Jack London, Archibald MacLeish, André Malraux (author of *The Human Condition*), W. Somerset Maugham, Alberto Moravia (Alberto Pincherle, author of *Man as an End*), Fridtjof Nansen, Llewelyn Powys, Romain Rolland, Ignazio Silone (Secondo Tranquilli), Wole Soyinka, Stephen Spender, Han Suyin, Rabindranath Tagore (Ravindranatha Thakura, author of *The Religion of Man*), Ernst Toller, Paul Valéry, Kurt Vonnegut, Angus Wilson, Marguerite Yourcenar (Marguerite de Crayencour), Stefan Zweig (author of *Great Moments of Mankind*), etc.

The term *aesthetic humanism* has occasionally been used for the particular attitude represented by artists and intellectuals who consciously adopted the traditions of classical Greece and Rome, the Renaissance and Romanticism, such as P. B. Shelley, Walter Pater, Oscar Wilde, Ernest Dowson, and the Bloomsbury Group (some of whom used the term).

A good example of cultural humanism in action is the monthly magazine *Horizon*, the leading British literary and artistic periodical published from the beginning of 1940 to the end of 1949. The editor Cyril Connolly contributed many remarkable "Comments." In the last issue (December 1949/January 1950), he said that one of his original purposes was "conserving the essential features of the heritage of Western humanism in time of danger." During the worst of that time (April 1941), he argued against all explicit ideologies but for an implicit ideology of humanism:

> Let this war be the end of the Ism, and serve to recreate from the humanity which is still so evident in small affairs and personal contacts a basis for future ideas of government. The Ism is a creation of the human mind which dominates its creator with a logic of its own until the commonlove and commonsense of humanity are destroyed by it. The love of power excludes the love of humanity, so does the love of order or of rigid intellectual systems, so that those at the top must be constantly irrigated from below. War has made us human and practical. We must enforce that change for the better, or be exterminated.

And when the war was over, he made explicit in one of his New Year resolutions the need "to work . . . for a new humanism which considers human life vulgar but sacred, and happiness, even of other people, as our supreme aim" (December 1945).

But in his famous farewell, which took "the message of the Forties" to be that "it is closing time in the gardens of the West," he seemed to have given up humanism as well as all the other isms in his final view of "man, betrayed by science, bereft of religion, deserted by the pleasant imaginings of humanism against the blind fate of which he is now so expertly conscious."

Religious Humanism

The words *humanist* and *humanism* in most of the senses so far mentioned have one unmistakable feature—a positive relationship with religion.

The original humanists of the Italian Renaissance were Christians who employed classical studies to rescue religion from medieval corruption. Their colleagues in other areas who were retrospectively described as humanists were Christians who based their emphasis on the human mind and body on the biblical doctrine that man had been created by God "in our image and likeness"; in 1486 the so-called oration *On the Dignity of Man* (*De dignitate hominis*) by Pico della Mirandola attributed the infinite possibilities of humanity to the gift of God, and in 1518 the *Fable of Man* (*Fabula de homine*) by Vives described the infinite ability of humanity as an imitation of the gods. The deists and theophilanthropists defended true religion against atheism. The educationists who defended humanism against philanthropinism or realism were Christians who emphasized the inclusion of Christianity as well as the classics in the curriculum. The Unitarians who emphasized the humanity of Jesus were attempting to rescue religion from the superhuman errors of Trinitarianism. The Humanitarians and Positivists were attempting to rescue religion from the superstitious errors of theology. The pragmatists were neither for nor against religion, but inclined at least as much to the former as to the latter position; James was sympathetic to mysticism and spiritualism, and Schiller's paper on "Science and Religion" for the Pan-Anglican Congress of 1908 claimed that humanism meant "the deepest and most thorough reconciliation of Science and Religion which it is possible to conceive" (*Pan-Anglican Papers*, 1908).

Christians have frequently pointed out that the original humanists were all Christians, and Catholics have correctly pointed out that most of them were actually Catholics. It should indeed be recognized that the Judaeo-Christian tradition has strong humanistic elements. Judaism is based on the doctrines that man was made in the image of God, and that some men have been chosen by God. Christianity is based on the doctrines of the Incarnation and the Trinity—that God has a *human* as well as a divine nature and consists of three persons, one of whom was his son Jesus, who became *man* to save *humanity*. (This is why it is blasphemous for both Jews and Muslims.) When meanings of humanism proliferated, several of them were specifically religious.

Devout humanism was applied to the seventeenth-century mystical tradition of Lessius and François de Sales. After the First World War there was a "Humanism of the Bible" series, and such books as *Evangelical Humanism* (1925) and *Studies in Old Testament Humanism* (1931).

Above all, the French neo-Thomist philosopher Jacques Maritain described his version of progressive Catholicism in his lectures of 1934 and his book of 1938 as *Humanisme intégral*—translated first as *True Humanism* (1938) and later as *Integral Humanism* (1973). He argued against both communist humanism and bourgeois humanism that "true humanism" or "authentic humanism" was based on classical and Christian elements, that "anthropocentric humanism" was "inhuman humanism," that what was needed was a "new humanism" based on Christianity and its doctrine of God made man. Such usage was followed by other Catholic intellectuals, especially in Latin countries (including several popes)—though it was dismissed by the historian G. G. Coulton as "an abuse of terms" (*Journal of the History of Ideas*, October 1944)—and in Britain by such figures as Christopher Dawson, Martin D'Arcy, and Bernard Wall.

The unorthodox Catholic evolutionism of the French biologist Pierre Teilhard de Chardin, especially in his posthumous book *Le Phénomène humain* (1959), translated as *The Phenomenon of Man* (1959), was often described as *humanism*, though not by him, and it influenced the evolutionary humanism of Julian Huxley. In the same way the *Personalism* of the French philosopher Emmanuel Mounier, which combined moderate Catholicism and moderate socialism with a touch of existentialism, was sometimes called *humanism*. Such unlikely Protestant figures as Karl Barth and Paul Tillich also claimed *Christian humanism*. Mircea Eliade the philosopher of religion sometimes claimed *new humanism*.

Martin Buber and Emmanuel Lévinas expressed different forms of *Jewish humanism*. In 1923 Buber wrote about *Ich und Du* (I and Thou). In 1972 Lévinas wrote about *Humanisme de l'autre homme* (Humanism of the Other Man), a form of altruistic humanism sometimes called *alter-humanism*; in 1974 he said that "humanism should be denounced only because it isn't human enough" in *Autrement qu'être, ou au-delà de l'essence* (Outside Being, or Beyond Essence). Albert Schweitzer called himself a humanist, though his principle of "reverence for life" (all life?) reduced the force of the term. The Quakerism of the Society of Friends is often close to humanism. There have been claims for Buddhist humanism and Islamic humanism. And the syncretic religion of Baha'i has also been described as humanism.

Humane Humanism

Meanwhile a curious byway was explored in Britain by a short-lived monthly paper called *The Humanist* (January 1924–August 1927), which after a couple of years was subtitled "A Journal for Progressive People."

This represented a form of upper-class humanitarianism rather than any recognizable kind of humanism. It was published at "Humanity House" in Westminster by the British Humane Association, "a non-religious and nonpolitical organization" founded in 1923 by Louis Campbell-Johnston and supported by "a group of businessmen," with the objects of "cooperation in all humane effort organized on sound business principles and the prevention of cruelty and suffering in all forms" and "civic self-development by spreading only ethical truth, as we hold that creeds and politics are a man's private affairs." Its motto was "Do unto others as you would they should do unto you," with the comment that "the law of God as laid down in the Golden Rule is a universal principle which ignores creed but recognizes—*Man*." It called for "the practical religion of social service" and added that "real religion is *living a life*." Its main practical interests were public health —especially ultraviolet treatment—and "social hygiene."

The Humanist tended to the extreme right in politics, opposing socialism except from above, and including such contributors as Henry Ford and Robert Baden-Powell. It seldom discussed humanism as such, though Julian Huxley contributed a characteristic letter defining humanism as "the aim of realizing the innate possibilities of human nature in the fullest and most all-round way," and Roger B. Lloyd contributed an article on "The Title Deeds of Humanism" (November 1925). He said: "Humanism is ultimately a philosophy and an attitude towards life. It is a philosophy that exalts man both as he is and as he might be." And he added: "There is no romance more exciting than the story of the rise of humanism." By this he meant mainly Renaissance humanism, especially Petrarch and Reuchlin. But other figures mentioned with admiration were Confucius and Mencius, Dante and Shakespeare, and a series of "Eminent Humanists" included Thomas Hardy, James Joyce, Bernard Shaw, G. K. Chesterton, John Galsworthy, and Liam O'Flaherty.

The Humanist tended to the extreme center in religion, with comments about "humanizing Religion" and "humanizing Humanity." A columnist with the pseudonym "The Traveller," who expounded "the philosophy of monism," wrote about "Humanism" (March 1926) and returned to the subject several times in 1927, linking what he called "Immanent Humanism" with what he called "Rational Christianity"— "a new era of Christianity . . . in which the humanist and the evangelist may lie down together" and the scientist and religionist may meet.

The Humanist soon ceased publication, because "the public will not read a propagandist paper," and the British Humane Association concentrated on its charitable activity.

The Humanist Movement

The modern humanist movement emerged during the mid-twentieth century, deriving from developments in both religious and nonreligious organizations, depending on the convergence of developments in the United States, Britain, the Netherlands, and India, and culminating in the establishment of an international organization after the Second World War.

Freethought and Humanism

Several other terms were used for and by our predecessors for a long time before the eventual adoption of *humanism*. During the eighteenth and nineteenth centuries, they were called infidels, unbelievers, deists, skeptics, atheists, and called themselves freethinkers, zetetics, cosmists, realists, naturalists or naturists, moralists, liberals, secularists, agnostics, ethicists or ethicalists, rationalists, monists. They experienced considerable difficulties with and exchanged continual dis-agreements about the meanings of these terms, and about the question whether they were religious or not.

Freethinkers generally used the words *humanist* and *humanism* in the same way as other people in the senses already described. Thus J. M. Robertson produced two books, based on lectures to the South Place Ethical Society, on "humanists"—writers who were not neces-sarily classical scholars or religious skeptics, but who were generally concerned with humanity. The first, which appeared in several editions from *Modern Humanists* (1891) to *Modern Humanists Reconsidered* (1927), covered Thomas Carlyle, John Stuart Mill, Ralph Waldo Emerson, Matthew Arnold, John Ruskin, Herbert Spencer; and the second, *Pioneer Humanists* (1907), covered Niccolò Machiavelli, Francis Bacon, Thomas Hobbes, Benedict Spinoza, Lord Shaftesbury, Bernard Mandeville, Edward Gibbon, and Mary Wollstonecraft.

Similarly A. W. Benn's *History of Modern Philosophy* (1912) ended with a chapter on "The Humanists of the Nineteenth Century," discussing philosophers of a similarly miscellaneous kind—Victor Cousin, Auguste Comte, John Stuart Mill, Herbert Spencer, several Hegelians, Rudolf Lotze and Eduard von Hartmann, and even Fried-rich Nietzsche and Henri Bergson.

The freethought movement was generally indifferent or opposed to *humanism* well into the twentieth century; but there were excep-tions, especially in the ethical movement (and to some extent in the rationalist movement) in Britain, and then in the Unitarian movement in the United States, and eventually the exceptions became the rule.

Ethicism and Rationalism

The Ethical movement of the late nineteenth century and early twen-tieth century played a small but significant part in the long journey from theistic religion to atheistic humanism. It attempted under the influence of Kant and Emerson to found a new religion based on belief in the objective existence and overriding importance of the Good or the Right, independent of any superhuman person or supernatural force. Ethical Culture Societies were formed on the initiative of Felix Adler in North America from 1876, Ethical Societies were formed on the initiative of Stanton Coit in Britain from 1886, and then similar societies were formed in several parts of continental Europe. National organizations were formed on both sides of the Atlantic during the 1890s, and an International Ethical Union in 1896.

Their members, who soon called themselves ethicists or ethical-ists, or ethical culturists, were close to and often involved in the rationalist movement, embodied from 1899 by the Rationalist Press Association (RPA), but they saw their organizations very definitely as religious societies, and considered that they were rescuing true religion from the metaphysical and moral errors of theism. Indeed the last such society in Britain, the South Place Ethical Society (which began in 1793 as a Universalist and Unitarian congregation and eventually became an Ethical Society in 1888), owned premises registered for religious worship until 1977 and claimed religious status until 1980, and still includes among its formal objects "the cultivation of a rational religious sentiment," although it has long been one of the main sections of the organized humanist movement.

And even when ethicists began to call themselves humanists, they originally meant it in a religious sense. Nevertheless it was from the ethical movement that the nonreligious philosophical sense of *humanism* gradually emerged in Britain, and it was from the convergence of the ethical and rationalist movements that this sense of *humanism* eventually prevailed throughout the freethought movement.

Several examples appeared in the paper of the Union of Ethical Societies, which was formed in 1896 on the initiative of Stanton Coit; this was published first as the *Ethical World* (January 1898–December 1900), then as *Democracy* (January–October 1901), *Ethics* (November 1901–March 1906), *Ethical Review* (March–October 1906), and again *Ethical World* (January 1907–June 1916). And a few examples appeared in Charles A. Watts's monthly and annual papers associated with the RPA—the *Literary Guide* (from November 1885), and the *Agnostic Annual* (1884–1907), *RPA Annual* (1908–1926), and *Rationalist Annual* (1927–1967).

To begin with, a counterexample—the first book published by the RPA, *The Religion of the Twentieth Century* (1899) by Joseph McCabe, a leading member of the ethical and rationalist movements from the 1890s to the 1950s. He stated that "the religion of the coming century" would be a "non-theological, or non-theistic, religion," a "purely human or ethical religion," an "ethical and purely human idealism," based on the "humanitarian ideal" or "humanitarian idea" or "humanitarian creed," as represented by the growing "humanitarian movement"; but he didn't call it *humanism*.

On the other hand, an example—an article called just "Humanism" by Charles E. Hooper, the first secretary of the RPA, published in the *Ethical World* as "the twentieth century is dawning" (December 8, 1900). He discussed the urgent need for reform in society, and listed the "three main parties of radical reformers"—the "intellectual reformers" (rationalists and secularists, subdivided into theists, atheists, pantheists, positivists, idealists, realists, and agnostics), whose ideal was "Truth"; the moral reformers (ethicists), whose ideal was "Worth"; and the "radical social reformers" (socialists, cooperators, trade unionists, and labor advocates), whose ideal was "Commonwealth." He argued that "organic reform" should be "intellectual, personal and social," and that the "ideal reformer"—the "most practical reformer," who would create "the New Humanity"—"must be at once a Rationalist, an Ethicist, and, in a broad sense, a Socialist." And he concluded with the first clear call in the freethought movement for the adoption of *humanism*:

> "Truth, Worth, Commonwealth." That, then, is the motto and brief symbol of the philosophy of reform which I have been trying to preach. But how to describe the philosophy itself? It is Humanism. The technical signifi-

cance which this term formerly possessed is practically forgotten. Latterly it has come into use in a sense somewhat vague, but, at the same time, nearly related to that which I propose to attach to it. *Humanism!* What one word could be better adapted to mark the gospel which is a gospel at once of human knowledge, of human nature, and of human society?

At the same time, Hooper contributed to the *Agnostic Annual* for 1901 an article on "Prospects and Problems of the Twentieth Century" in which he called on rationalists to work not only for "humanist ethics" but for "a humanist religion." A few years later he called in *Ethics* for a new "Religion of Humanity" (July 15, 1907); and at the end of his life he wrote in the *Literary Guide* advocating "Rational Humanism" (November 1931) and suggesting that the RPA should adopt humanism "as its practical ideal."

Back in 1902, when for the first time a secularist leader (Charles Watts) spoke to an Ethical Society (St. Pancras), Coit emphasized the significance of the event, and expressed the hope that "in another generation there will not be various movements appearing more or less as factions and rivals in the cause of democracy and ethical rationalism, but that all these forces will become conscious of their kinship, and become knit together and unified in one powerful and efficient organization," so that instead of separate secularists, socialists, free-thinkers, rationalists, positivists, individualists, cooperators, "these shall all be one" (May 13, 1902). He didn't suggest what their unifying principle should be, but he supposed that they would begin by joining the Union of Ethical Societies.

Other people also did so. In 1906 the philosopher J. S. Mackenzie, who was a leading member of the ethical movement, gave the Dunkin Lectures at Manchester College, Oxford, published as *Lectures on Humanism* (1907). He distinguished humanism both from Schiller's pragmatism and from mere naturalism, emphasizing the concentration on humanity and anticipating the later conception of humanism, though he emphasized its practical manifestation in "Ethical religion" as practiced in ethical societies.

A letter from Charles J. Whitby questioned "The Designation of the Ethical Movement" (September 15, 1907):

> I believe the word in use is in many ways unsatisfactory, and I suggest the title *Humanist* as an unexceptionable alternative. . . . Humanism is the religion of all great poetry and art, the religion of science and philosophy, and is nothing if not ethical.

Coit replied that, while he liked the term "more and more" and used it in his new book *National Idealism and a State Church* (1907), it was unsuitable for the title of a movement, partly because "within humanism there are many points of view," and partly because it could be nonethical or even antiethical (November 15, 1907). Ironically, C. T. Gorham's obituary of the great South Place minister Moncure Conway in the following issue was headlined "A Great Humanist" (December 15, 1907). But *humanism* could never become the rubric of the Ethical movement while it was led by Coit, who always stressed its religious features, even using the word *God*, and ran the Ethical Church in West London from 1909 onward.

A few years later, however, when his paper ceased publication it was succeeded by a new "Organ of the Ethical Movement" called simply *The Humanist* (January 1917–March 1923). The main editor was George A. Smith of the North London Ethical Society (one of his coeditors was C. T. Gorham, the second secretary of the RPA). The first issue opened with a front-page editorial on "The Religion of Humanism" based on "faith in man," and followed with Harry Snell's claim that "We Are All Humanists Now"; Smith wrote many more articles which were reprinted in his pamphlet *A Humanist Religion* (1920) and in his book *Little Essays in Religion* (1923), repeatedly referring to "the Religion of Humanism."

The legal scholar Roland K. Wilson at the very end of his life described "Humanism: An Experiment in Religion" in the *Hibbert Journal* (October 1919). He discussed the various words used for freethinkers, and commented:

But the term Humanism seems the aptest to express the constructive affir-
mation, taken from one of the manifestoes of the Union of Ethical Societies, that "moral ideas and the moral life are not necessarily dependent
on beliefs as to the ultimate nature of things, and as to a life after death."

He distinguished "our Ethical Humanism" from both Renaissance humanism and pragmatism, described it as an "experiment in religion,"
and suggested that "Humanism is, and is likely to be for a long time to
come, an experiment needing very careful handling and much courage
and wisdom in its votaries, in order to give it a fair chance of success."
He added: "I think it must be admitted that in a purely Humanistic
society there would be some changes in our estimate of moral values;
but I see no reason to suppose that the changes would on the whole be
for the worse." And he concluded:

Faith is indispensable, for Humanism as for every other religion, but not
as a substitute for knowledge; rather in the sense of willingness to take
risks for a worthy object, where certainty is unattainable; also in the sense
of loyalty to the principle of human brotherhood, even where the price to
be paid in personal suffering is not a matter of risk but of certainty.

A key figure in this process was F. J. Gould, who was an active
member of many progressive movements and a regular contributor to
many progressive papers for half a century, from the 1880s to the
1930s, especially as the leading theoretician and practitioner of moral
education in schools, and also as a founder and the first historian of the
RPA. He said in the *Literary Guide* that "true Rationalism includes
Humanism" (October 1900), and added: "I am a Freethinker, Atheist,
Agnostic, Secularist, Positivist, Ethicist, Rationalist" (November
1900); he was also a Marxist, and he increasingly called himself a
humanist and used the word *humanism* to express the combination of
all these ideas. Thus he contributed to a symposium on "The Future of
Religion" in the *Agnostic Annual* for 1900:

A new ideal is actually displacing Theism, and it is the growth of this
new ideal which explains latter-day scepticism. What is the new ideal?
Conveniently, though not perhaps picturesquely, it may be described as
humanism. The point suggested by the employment of the word
"humanism" lies in the contrast with Theism. Silently, and almost
imperceptibly, the religious temper is transferring its admiration from
the divine to the manly and womanly.

Gould later published his autobiography as *The Life-Story of a
Humanist* (1923), and for the rest of his life he used *humanism* by
preference. S. H. Swinny, president of the London Positivist Society
and editor of the *Positivist Review*, preceded his review of the book
with "Humanism . . . A Note on the Word" (June 1923). He noted that
Humanist was used "as an alternative" to *Positivist* and commented
that "we are both Humanists and Positivists," but added that "we certainly claim no proprietary right in the word *Humanist*" and that "we
welcome all to the Humanist name," complained about Schiller's
attempt to restrict its use to his version of pragmatism, and welcomed
its growing use by ethicists. After Swinny's death, Gould took over the
Positivist Review in January 1924, changing its name to *Humanity* (it
closed in December 1925).

At the same time he wrote in the *Literary Guide* on "Rationalism
in 1950" (January 1924), discussing "the task for Rationalism and for
Humanism" and repeatedly referring to "the Humanist movement."
He welcomed the "New Humanism" of the rising movement in the
United States (September 1931), and hailed the "Humanist Woman"
(March 1935). Among his last publications were a *Humanist Pro-
gramme of Life and Progress* (1932) and a leaflet on *The Humanist
Tomorrow* (1936). And his final contribution to the *Rationalist Annual*
(1937) included a reference to his lifelong observation of "the lines of
theological decline and of humanist progress." He was disappointed
that much of his work seemed to have got nowhere, but at least in this
direction it got there in the end.

There were other influential voices in those days steadily pushing freethinkers toward *humanism*, even in the rationalist movement. Charles A. Watts preferred *rationalism*, but he referred in the *RPA Annual* for 1917 to "the Humanist gospel." Joseph McCabe also preferred *rationalism*, but he wrote in the *RPA Annual* for 1915 about "the Humanism which is displacing Christianity in ruling the minds of men." C. T. Gorham similarly wrote in the *RPA Annual* for 1918 about the "spirit of Humanism."

The social scientist J. A. Hobson, who was a leading ethicist and was described by his friend H. N. Brailsford as "a rationalist and a humanist to the core," tried to introduce humanist ideas into his pioneering work in economics and sociology, and also tried to establish the word *humanism* in such studies. He argued in *God and Mammon* (1931) for "a definitely human religion," "an organized ethical religion" and "a rationalist religion," which he called "Humanism." And he took as the subject of his Conway Memorial Lecture *Rationalism and Humanism* (1933), calling for "Rationalists to count themselves as Humanists" and for "the reconcilement of rationalism and humanism" through the ethical movement.

Hobson also added a rather lighter touch. Writing about "The Ethical Movement and the Natural Man" in the *Hibbert Journal* (July 1922), he asked, "Do we want to claim the title *Humanist*, indicating that the whole of Humanity is our concern?" and commented:

> Now the natural man is a little suspicious of these large unfamiliar terms, and is apt to direct against them a quality which humanists could do well to take into account because its name should recommend it to them, the quality of Humor. For the natural man is certainly a bit of a humorist, and claims for Humor a definite and considerable place in life. Now this humor is particularly directed against persons whose language or bearing indicate that they take themselves too seriously.

This lesson was not taken as seriously as it should have been.

The scholar and politician Gilbert Murray advocated a form of humanism based on classical ideas and combining liberalism and positivism, ethicism and rationalism, which opposed both theism and what he called the "Satanism" of the modern age. In his Conway Memorial Lecture *Myths and Ethics, or Humanism and the World's Need* (1944), he described the various kinds of freethinkers and rejected their existing titles:

> If we seek a name by which to denote these separate uncoordinated individuals, perhaps the most convenient is to call them *Humanists*. . . . By a Humanist I mean essentially one who accepts it as the special duty of Man, whether he has a "Friend behind phenomena" or not, to raise life to some higher level and redeem the world from its misery.

And his posthumous collection was called *Humanist Essays* (1964).

Scientific Humanism

One of the most important factors in the adoption of *humanism* as a clearly nonreligious or antireligious term was the enormous growth in the theoretical and practical power of science and technology, the explicit application of the ideology of science and technology to the interests of humanity, and the use of the word *humanism* to convey this meaning. In one way science had demoted humanity, by removing the Earth from the center of the universe and man from the top of the tree of life; but in another way science had promoted humanity, by providing human beings with greater knowledge about and control over their species and their planet.

John Morley, the liberal journalist and politician, who sympathized with positivism and anticipated the decline and fall of theistic religion in *On Compromise* (1874), insisted that it must be replaced by a new faith, which would be based on science but would draw on traditional beliefs, and would show some of the negative aspects of such beliefs:

Science, when she has accomplished all her triumphs in her own order, will still have to go back, when the time comes, to assist in the building up of a new creed by which man can live. . . . It can hardly be other than an expansion, a development, a re-adaptation, of all the moral and spiritual truth that lay hidden under the worn-out forms. . . . The future faith, like that of the past, brings not peace but a sword. It is a tale, not of concord, but of households divided against themselves.

He based such a faith on pity, justice, and progress. He didn't mention humanism, though in "Liberalism and Reaction" (1904) he recommended "the plain humanistic rationalistic way of looking at life and its problems."

Ernst Haeckel, the German advocate of Darwinism (and inventor of ecology in 1866), advocated a religion of nature called *monism* (similar to Holyoake's *Cosmism*), but he opposed what he called *anthropism*—"that powerful and world-wide group of erroneous opinions which opposes the human organism to the whole of the rest of nature, and represents it to be the preordained end of the organic creation, an entity essentially distinct from it, a god-like being" in *Systematic Phylogeny* (1895).

In *Die Welträthsel* (1899), translated as *The Riddle of the Universe* (1900), he explained his criticism of the three dogmas of anthropism: the *anthropocentric* dogma, which "culminates in the idea that man is the preordained centre and aim of all terrestrial life—or, in the wider sense, of the whole universe"; the *anthropomorphic* dogma, which "likens the creation and control of the world by God to the artificial creation of a talented engineer or mechanic, and to the administration of a wise ruler"; and the *anthropolatric* dogma, which "naturally results from this comparison of the activity of God and man; it ends in the apotheosis of the human organism." Such ideas appeared in several forms of religious and spiritual humanism, and have reappeared in some forms of the so-called "Anthropic Principle."

The idea of a "new" humanism which would embody a faith based on science seems to have come to several people quite independently.

When the American botanist Luther Burbank openly declared himself an "infidel" in 1926, just before his death, he demanded the replacement of traditional religion based on the God of the Bible with a "Religion of Humanity" based on the "God of Science."

When George Sarton, the historian of science (and father of the writer May Sarton), was living in Belgium before he emigrated to the United States he produced a pamphlet called *The Faith of a Humanist* (1912), and described his ideas as "New Humanism" in 1918. He later wrote *The History of Science and the New Humanism* (1931), attempting to unite the "old humanism" of literary culture with scientific culture:

> The New Humanism is a double renaissance: a scientific renaissance for men of letters, and a literary one for men of science. . . . We must prepare a new culture, the first to be deliberately based upon science, upon humanized science—the New Humanism.

When Bronisław Malinowski, the Polish anthropologist who founded the modern science of social anthropology, was doing fieldwork in the Trobriand Islands during the First World War, he wrote in his diary—published posthumously as *A Diary in the Strict Sense of the Term* (1967)—about his ideas for a "New Humanism." He felt that "humanistic thinking" was "profound and important" and that it was a "fatal error" to link it to the classics, and he planned to write about "the essence of humanism" and to "sketch a new plan in which living man, living language, and living full-blooded facts would be the core of the situation" (April 1918). In his Riddell Lectures of 1935, published as *The Foundations of Faith and Morals* (1936), he remarked that "even an agnostic has to live by faith," in his case "the faith in humanity and its power of improvement," however much this had been shaken by world war and dictatorship.

During the early twentieth century humanists who were concerned with science and scientists who were concerned with humanity adopted the term *scientific humanism* to express their common view. Such people were generally liberals or socialists, or—as the rival dogmas of fascism and communism came to dominate the world between the world wars—increasingly Communists. Thus in Sweden a *Humanist Manifesto* (1919), signed by scores of scientists and socialists, appeared in Ivan Oljelund's *Humanismen: Nagra Synpunkter* (Humanism: Some Views). In the United States, Lothrop Stoddard advocated *scientific humanism* (1926) as "a new Renaissance," Henry C. Tracy published *Towards the Open* (1927), subtitled "A Preface to Scientific Humanism," and Leon Samson in *The New Humanism* (1930) supported "scientific humanism" in the sense of "dialectical materialism."

During the early 1930s there were several attempts to persuade the existing freethought organizations to abandon their traditional secularism or rationalism or ethicism in favor of scientific humanism, with a strong bias toward the political left. Thus in the *Literary Guide* J. B. Coates argued that the RPA should adopt *scientific humanism* (August 1931), only to receive a generally hostile response, including a crushing rebuke from the veteran rationalist, J. M. Robertson (October 1931). Similar suggestions were proposed and rejected in the other sections of the freethought movement; the result was the formation in 1932 of the Federation of Progressive Societies and Individuals (from 1940 the Progressive League), whose leaders—such as C. E. M. Joad —played a part in the continuing advocacy of scientific humanism.

A mark of the advance of *scientific humanism* in Britain between the world wars was the short-lived monthly paper *The Realist* (April 1929–January 1930), which was subtitled "A Journal of Scientific Humanism." It was edited by Archibald Church, with a board including Arnold Bennett, George Catlin, Richard Gregory, J. B. S. Haldane, Gerald Heard, Aldous and Julian Huxley, Harold Laski, Bronisław Malinowski, Naomi Mitchison, Herbert Read, and H. G. Wells. Its articles on "Scientific Humanism" by Charles Singer (April 1929) and Lancelot Hogben (December 1929) said much about science and little about humanism, and seemed to mark the conquest of traditional humanism by modern science.

The popular symposium *What I Believe* (1938) included several freethinkers, but only Hogben actually described his belief as *humanism*, reprinting his contribution as "The Creed of a Scientific Humanist" in his collection of *Dangerous Thoughts* (1939). A similar symposium, also called *What I Believe* (1947), also included several freethinkers, but again only Ivor Brown described his belief as *humanism*.

A crucial figure in the development of the humanist movement was the British biologist Julian Huxley, arguing first for *scientific humanism* and then for *evolutionary humanism*, and always for a humanist "religion." In his autobiographical *Memories* (1970) he told how he was converted to scientific humanism by reading John Morley and to religious humanism by reading Mrs. Humphry Ward (his aunt). In *Essays of a Biologist* (1923) he called for a new religion based on science. He spoke to the Annual Dinner of the RPA in 1926, calling for "a humanism that is both reasonable and rationalist" (*Literary Guide*, July 1926).

He wrote a book on *Religion Without Revelation* (1927), introducing the first edition:

> Man can and should begin constructing a new common outlook, a new habitation for his spirit, new from the foundations up, on the basis of a scientific humanism.

He defined "the idea of humanism" as "human control by human effort in accordance with human ideals," and concluded that it was "the religion of life." His Conway Memorial Lecture *Science, Religion, and Human Nature* (1930) similarly called for a new "religion of life," "a religion based on science and human nature." *What Dare I Think* (1931), described as "Essays in Scientific Humanism," included the Conway Memorial Lecture and also the Henry La Barre Jayne lectures for 1931 calling for *scientific humanism*. *The Uniqueness of Man* (1940) included a chapter explaining "Scientific Humanism":

> Scientific humanism is a protest against supernaturalism: the human spirit, now in its individual, now in its corporate aspects, is the source

of all values and the highest reality we know. It is a protest against one-sidedness and fixity: the human spirit has many sides and cannot be ruled by any single rule.

And he called for formal organizations to put it into practice, and mentioned what he called "universalist Humanism." In the second edition of *Religion Without Revelation* (1941), he looked forward to "a socially-grounded humanist religion" and to "the rise of humanist religions to pre-eminence." In the 1945 *Rationalist Annual* he discussed "Religion and Humanism." In *New Bottles for New Wine* (1957) he called for "Transhumanism"—with the claim that "the human species can, if it wishes, transcend itself . . . in its entirety, as humanity"—and for "Evolutionary Humanism."

Aldous Huxley had meanwhile followed Gerald Heard to the United States and into mysticism, and later described his philosophy as a "pessimistic humanism"!

A characteristic attempt to combine scientific and religious humanism was made at the beginning of the Second World War by Lewis Manikin in his pamphlet *Scientific Humanism, or The Religion of Humanity* (1940), which advocated "a loftier, more significant and more constructive philosophy," called "scientific humanism," argued that "the only religion which can serve as a basis for modern culture is the absolute religion; the religion of humanity," and still included the idea of God. This ambitious but ambiguous appeal had little impact.

American Unitarianism

The decisive factor in the emergence of a permanent movement which called itself *humanist* was a uniquely American process, following a characteristic tradition in the United States of radical developments in religion, and consisting of the convergence of moderate believers and moderate unbelievers seeking common ground. This tendency had led

in the late nineteenth century to the formation of the short-lived Free
Religious Association, and it led in the early twentieth century to the
longer-lasting emergence of a humanist faction within the Unitarian
denomination, beginning at the time of the First World War.

Unitarianism is an inherently unstable position, and during the
nineteenth century many American Unitarians followed the path from
belief toward unbelief, from a "credal" to a "noncredal" position—as
had the British Unitarians of the South Place Chapel in London, who
left the Unitarian denomination during the 1830s, moved away from
theism toward humanism from the 1860s to the 1880s, and became an
Ethical Society in 1888.

In the much larger Unitarian denomination in the United States,
W. C. Gannett's influential statement of *The Things Most Commonly
Believed To-Day Among Us* (1887), which barely united warring factions, included belief in God only at the very end. Many Unitarians,
especially in the Midwest, began to go further. Having discarded the
second and third persons of the Trinity, they discarded the first person
too, replacing supernaturalism and theism with naturalism and
humanism. Although they ceased to believe in God, they continued to
call themselves religious, and mostly to count themselves as Unitarians, but increasingly to adopt the term *humanism*. Between the two
world wars, about one-tenth of the Unitarian denomination became
humanists, and there was a danger of schism between "God Men" and
"No God Men"; but first the humanists began to leave, and then the
latter began to adopt humanism as well. (The official principles of the
American Unitarian Universalist Alliance, which united the two denominations in 1961, include both God and humanism, and more than
half its members now call themselves humanists.)

This movement was initiated by a few individuals who had themselves only recently left other denominations and become Unitarian
ministers—John H. Dietrich in 1911, Curtis W. Reese in 1913, and
Charles F. Potter in 1914—and it became public when Dietrich and
Reese met at the Western Unitarian Conference in Des Moines, Iowa,

in 1917. The subsequent development was punctuated by successive publications rejecting theistic and transcendental in favor of naturalistic and secular beliefs, and employing the terms *humanist* or *humanism*. Frank C. Doan, another Unitarian minister, had already defended "modernism" and "humanism" in *Religion and the Modern Mind* (1909). The philosopher Roy Wood Sellars wrote *The Next Step in Religion: An Essay Toward the Coming Renaissance* (1918), the last chapter of which was "The Humanist's Religion":

> The Humanist's religion is the religion of one who says yea to life here and now, of one who is self-reliant, intelligent and creative. It is the religion of the will to power, of one who is hard on himself and yet joyous in himself. It is the religion of courage and purpose and transforming energy.

His *Evolutionary Naturalism* (1922) provided the philosophical basis for the new religion. His *Religion Coming of Age* (1928) looked forward to a "New Reformation" as well as a "New Renaissance," and expected that "Christianity will gradually be transformed" into "humanistic religion," "a religion founded on realities in a religion coming of age." Mangasar Mangasarian, an ethical leader who led an Independent Religious Society in Chicago from 1900, wrote *Humanism, a Religion for Americans* (1925).

Dietrich gave a series of sermons which were broadcast on the radio and published under the general title *The Humanist Pulpit* (1926–1933). Reese published *Humanism* (1926) and *Humanist Religion* (1931). In the latter he said that humanism is "a philosophy of human control in contrast with all form of fatalistic determination as applied to human situations." He later wrote *The Meaning of Humanism* (1945). He edited a collection of *Humanist Sermons* (1928) by eighteen Unitarian and other ministers. Among them Doan just spoke on "Just Being Human" and E. Burdette Backus concluded:

> Humanity has struck its tents and is again on the march towards a new religious faith . . . though I am keenly aware that that which I call

religion will seem to many earnest men and women not religion at all,
but rather irreligion.

A particularly influential figure was A. Eustace Haydon at the University of Chicago:

> The humanist has a feeling of perfect at-homeness in the universe. He
> is conscious of himself as an earth child. There is a mystic glow in this
> sense of belonging. . . . Rooted in millions of years of planetary history,
> he has a secure feeling of being at home, and a consciousness of pride
> and dignity as a bearer of the heritage of the ages and a growing creative
> center of cosmic life.

He encouraged the formation in 1927 of a humanist fellowship among teachers and students at Chicago University, which began a paper called *New Humanist* (April 1928–September/October 1936, first duplicated and then printed from November 1930). The publishers called themselves the New Humanist Associates, and from 1935 the Humanist Press Association (on the model of the Rationalist Press Association). In California, Theodore C. Abell led the Unitarian Society of Hollywood, publishing the *Hollywood Humanist* (1927–1933), A. D. Faupel led the Fellowship of Humanity in Oakland, and Lowell H. Coate led the Humanistic Society of Friends in Los Angeles.

In 1929 Potter left the Unitarians and founded the "First Humanist Society" in New York (which was supported by Dewey and also by Will Durant, Helen Keller, and James Leuba). He published *Humanism: A New Religion* (1930) and *Humanizing Religion* (1933); in the former he claimed:

> Humanism is not simply another denomination of Protestant Chris-
> tianity; it is not a creed; nor is it a cult. It is a new type of religion alto-
> gether. . . . The chief concern of Humanism is to release the pent-up
> reservoir of human energy, to cultivate the neglected garden of the
> mind, and to raise to its highest efficiency the entire personality. . . . If
> humanists were to make a creed, the first article would be—I believe in
> Man.

Oliver R. Reiser published *Humanistic Logic* (1930) and *Humanism and New World Ideals* (1933). He later turned to "super-humanism" in *The Promise of Scientific Humanism* (1940) and *Scientific Humanism: A Formulation* (1943), and then to *Cosmic Humanism* (1966) and *Cosmic Humanism and World Unity* (1975). Joseph Walker published *Humanism as a Way of Life* (1932), "an attempt briefly to set forth a sound philosophy of life and a religion without supernaturalism or superstition," based on a personal humanistic religion. Gordon Kent, who led a humanist society in Moline, Illinois, produced several editions of *Humanism for the Millions*.

There were similarities with and connections between the new humanists and the older ethicists, though they were separated by the Christian character of the former and the Jewish character of the latter. A significant event—coinciding with the death of Felix Adler, the founder of the ethical movement—was the appearance of *A Humanist Manifesto* (first published in the *New Humanist*, May/June 1933, and widely reprinted), initiated by Raymond B. Bragg, drafted by Sellars, organized by Edwin H. Wilson, and signed by thirty-four intellectuals, mostly Unitarians, but also Universalists, ethicists, and progressive Jews, as well as publicists, publishers, and philosophers (including Dewey). It began:

> The time has come for widespread recognition of the radical changes in religious beliefs throughout the modern world. The time is past for mere revision of traditional attitudes. Science and economic change have disrupted the old beliefs. Religions the world over are under the necessity of coming to terms with new conditions created by a vastly increased knowledge and experience. In every field of human activity, the vital movement is now in the direction of a candid and explicit humanism.

And it presented fifteen theses of "religious humanism," rejecting theism and supernaturalism and affirming a combination of liberalism and socialism. It cautiously avoided attempting any definition of *humanism*.

This episode had considerable impact in the United States in the period of fear and hope during the Depression and the New Deal, and the twin threats of dictatorship and war, and developments continued to follow rapidly. Another significant event was Dewey's influential Terry Lectures, published as *A Common Faith* (1934), which appealed for a shared belief which was *religious*, though not a *religion*:

> The ideal ends to which we attach our faith are not shadowy and wavering. They assume concrete form in our understanding of our relations to one another and the values contained in these relations. We who now live are parts of a humanity that extends into the remote past, a humanity that has interacted with nature. The things in civilization we most prize are not of ourselves. They exist by grace of the doings and sufferings of the continuous human community in which we are a link. Ours is the responsibility of conserving, transmitting, rectifying and expanding the heritage of values we have received that those who come after us may receive it more solid and secure, more widely accessible and more generously shared than we have received it. Here are the elements for a religious faith that shall not be confined to sect, class, or race. Such a faith has always been implicitly the common faith of mankind. It remains to make it explicit and militant.

He didn't explicitly describe it as *humanism*, but many other people did so.

J. A. C. F. Auer gave the Lowell Lectures for 1932, published as *Humanism States Its Case* (1933), in which he stated that, while old humanism looked backward and tried to revive old values, "twentieth century humanism looks forward, creating its values as it progresses" —though he admitted that "it is a new thing, and it would be better served if we could find a new name for it." With Julian Hartt he later published *Humanism versus Theism* (1941). S. H. Jones published *Humanism* (1936). There were also attacks on this growing form of humanism, such as Charles Hartshorne's *Beyond Humanism* (1937), which advocated "a philosophical movement" which would be "a genuine integration (for the first time) of all the modern motifs," in opposition to "its great contemporary rival, humanism."

In 1934 the publishers of *New Humanist* formed the American Humanist Association (AHA). This circulated a *News Letter* and then the *Humanist Bulletin* (December 1938–January 1941), and finally launched a permanent magazine called *The Humanist* (April 1941), whose first issue included Sellars's article on "Humanism as a Religion," based on "an integral and humanistic naturalism." The AHA was incorporated in 1941, and it steadily expanded during and after the Second World War, exploiting its success by calling for European and international organizations to adopt *humanism*. It took a leading part in developing humanist principles and in encouraging humanist organizations in other countries, and in working for the establishment of an international humanist organization.

Naturalistic Humanism

Between the world wars *humanism* became a fashionable word in the United States, used in several religious, literary, political, and scientific senses, with confusing results. The chapter on "The Paradox of Humanism" in Joseph Wood Krutch's book *The Modern Temper* (1929) remarked that "it has been most frequently employed rather because of certain affective connotations than because of any exact meaning." Clarification was offered by two intellectuals from Columbia University.

The mathematician Cassius J. Keyser discussed the situation in his book *Humanism and Science* (1931); a digest appeared as "Humanism and Pseudo-Humanism" in the *Hibbert Journal* (January 1931). He expounded a version of scientific humanism, without actually using the term, stressing his allegiance to both science and humanism, and proclaiming that "the spirit of Science" is "the soul of Humanism."

He dismissed most of the current interpretations of *humanism*:

> No one can examine the recent American output of literature purporting to disclose the nature of Humanism without discovering that the writers, having employed the term in a large variety of incompatible senses,

agree in nothing save their appropriation, or misappropriation, of a common name.

In the *Hibbert Journal* he added that as a result "there are humanisms and humanisms and humanisms"!

He suggested that *humanism* is "a great name—among the greatest of our English speech," but he rejected most of the proposed versions as "Pseudo-Humanism" because he considered that they were not really humanist. He included in this category the religious humanism of the radical Unitarians, objecting that for them "religion is not good because it is humanism but humanism is good because it is religion." He rejected any attempt at definition, commenting that *humanism* "must be regarded as one of the great indefinables of our English speech," and preferred description, approvingly quoting Lippmann's usage. And he offered the following description of *humanism* in both negative and positive aspects:

> Not the intention of depraved men to escape, by humble submission to ecclesiastical authority and by means of divine grace, from the eternal wrath of an angry God; not the intention of superstitious men to propitiate, by purchase or prayer or sacrifice, the countless malignant spirits of an imaginary environment; not the intention of dupes to submit supinely to the indignities of the present world in the hope of everlasting bliss in a world beyond the grave; but the intention of perfectly natural men to "concern themselves with the discovery"—or, as I should prefer to say, with the creation—"of a good life" here upon this mundane sphere where they actually live, and to do it by the application of native powers resident in themselves to the waiting resources of the actual world.

He emphasized "a very precious and very powerful human sense":

> I mean the sense that humans are, as humans, naturally endowed with the dignity of autonomous beings, potentially qualified by native inheritance to judge, individually and independently, for themselves, in all the great matters of human concern, and, by the exercise of their own faculties, to order and fashion their lives worthily.

> The living sense of personal autonomy is absolutely essential to the proper dignity of man as man. Whenever and wherever it has been keenly felt, Humanism has flourished. Whenever and wherever it has been dormant or dead, Humanism has declined or perished. It is from the living sense in men of their personal autonomy that Humanism derives its existence, its character and its power.

And he described "the dream of modern Humanism":

> The concept of Humanism has not been a fixed, hardened, static thing but an enlarging function of time and experience. Compared with the Humanism of antiquity and even with that of the Renaissance, the Humanism of today is far more embracing, richer and more enlightened, owing to the increase within it of two momentous elements, which were not indeed wholly absent in the elder days but were then present only dimly, sporadically, embryonically. I refer to an Insight and a Belief.

The former was that "the insight that individual life and community life are so functionally related to one another, so essentially interdependent, that an endeavor to achieve a good individual life without concern for community well-being is futile and blind"; and the latter was "the belief in the endless progressibility of mankind, in the endless ameliorability of societal institutions, in the unlimited perfectibility of human weal."

> And so it has come about that the Dream of dreams of modern civilized man is Humanism's dream of world unity, world solidarity and world cooperation, to be more and more approximated by means discoverable by human faculties.

This broad view of humanism was supported by the American philosopher Corliss Lamont. He argued that humanism was not a religion or a sect or a cult, but a philosophy, which he called *naturalistic humanism* (sometimes *cultural humanism*); he wrote many articles and gave many lectures on the subject, and eventually put his work together in *Humanism as a Philosophy* (1949), republished in many later editions as *The Philosophy of Humanism*.

Lamont proposed a set of "principal propositions in the humanist philosophy." The original version appeared in "The Meaning of Humanism" (American *Humanist*, Summer 1942):

> First, a belief, based mainly on the sciences of biology, psychology and medicine, that man is an evolutionary product of the nature that is his home and an inseparable unity of body and personality having no possibility of individual immortality.
>
> Second, a metaphysics or world-view that rules out all forms of the supernatural and that regards the universe as a dynamic and constantly changing system of events which exists independently of any mind or consciousness and which follows a regular cause-effect sequence everywhere and at all times.
>
> Third, a conviction that man has the capacity and intelligence successfully to solve his own problems and that he should rely on reason and scientific method to do so.
>
> Fourth, an ethics that holds as its highest aim the this-earthly happiness, freedom and progress, both economic and cultural, of all humanity, regardless of nation or race, religion or occupation, sex or age.
>
> Fifth, a far-reaching social program that stands for the establishment throughout the world of peace and democracy as the foundations of a cooperative economic order, both national and international.

The final version appeared in the sixth edition of *The Philosophy of Humanism* (1982):

> First, Humanism believes in a naturalistic metaphysics or attitude toward the universe that considers all forms of the supernatural as myth; and that regards Nature as the totality of being and as a constantly changing system of matter and energy which exists independently of any mind or consciousness.
>
> Second, Humanism, drawing especially upon the laws and facts of science, believes that man is an evolutionary product of the Nature of which he is part; that his mind is indivisibly conjoined with the functioning of his brain; and that as an inseparable unity of body and personality he can have no conscious survival after death.

Third, Humanism, having its ultimate faith in man, believes that human beings, while conditioned by the past, possess the power or potentiality of solving their own problems, through reliance primarily upon reason and scientific method applied with courage and vision.

Fourth, Humanism, in opposition to all theories of universal determinism, fatalism, or predestination, believes that human beings, while conditioned by the past, possess genuine freedom of creative choice and action, and are, within certain objective limits, the masters of their own destiny.

Fifth, Humanism believes in an ethics or morality that grounds all human values in this-earthly experiences and relationships and that holds as its highest goal the this-worldly happiness, freedom, and progress—economic, cultural, and ethical—of all mankind, irrespective of nation, race, or religion.

Sixth, Humanism believes that the individual attains the good life by harmoniously combining personal satisfactions and continuous self-development with significant work and other activities that contribute to the welfare of the community.

Seventh, Humanism believes in the widest possible development of art and the awareness of beauty, including the appreciation of Nature's loveliness and splendor, so that the aesthetic experience may become a pervasive reality in the life of man.

Eighth, Humanism believes in a far-reaching social program that stands for the establishment throughout the world of democracy, peace, and a high standard of living on the foundations of a flourishing economic order, both national and international.

Ninth, Humanism believes in the complete social implementation of reason and scientific method, and thereby in democratic procedures, and parliamentary government, with full freedom of expression and civil liberties, throughout all areas of economic, political, and cultural life.

Tenth, Humanism, in accordance with scientific method, believes in the unending questioning of basic assumptions and convictions, including its own. Humanism is not a new dogma, but is a developing philosophy ever open to experimental testing, newly discovered facts, and more rigorous reasoning.

This clearly secularist and vaguely socialist version of humanism became increasingly influential in the new humanist movement (despite Lamont's reputation as a Communist fellow-traveller), and drew it steadily away from old-time religion and toward the old freethought movement. As a result, the American Humanist Association continued to prosper after the Second World War, during the period of renewed doubt and fear of the cold war and McCarthyism, battles over civil rights, and the rise of the so-called Moral Majority. It took a leading part in the establishment of an international humanist movement, and the American *Humanist* became a leading paper of the international humanist press.

The fortieth anniversary of the original *Humanist Manifesto* was marked by the appearance of *Humanist Manifesto II* (first published in the *Humanist*, September/October 1973, and widely reprinted). This was drafted by the philosopher Paul Kurtz and signed by hundreds of intellectuals of all kinds. It contained seventeen much longer points, and tried to cover much more ground in support of its opening statement that "the next century can and should be the humanistic century." Like its predecessor, it didn't attempt to define *humanism*, whether religious or nonreligious. Unlike its predecessor, it didn't affirm religion, nor even religious humanism; but neither did it reject religion, although it did deny supernaturalism and theism. It named several "varieties and emphases of naturalistic humanism"—scientific, ethical, democratic, religious, Marxist—and it embraced several other ideologies—"free thought, atheism, agnosticism, skepticism, deism, rationalism, ethical culture, and liberal religion."

British Humanism I

Such developments helped to foster the emergence of a specifically humanist movement in Britain immediately after the Second World War.

The establishment of rival right-wing and left-wing dictatorships around the world, the experiences of world war and cold war, the decline of religious and political orthodoxy—all encouraged a climate in which the various strands of freethought could converge and unite into a new movement, and the term *humanism* seemed increasingly appropriate for it. This applied in many parts of Europe; in 1946 the French writer Fernand Robert said in *L'Humanisme: Essai de défini-tion* (Humanism: Attempt at Definition), "At the end of the Second World War, the word *humanism* is in fashion." In Britain few individuals and small organizations were involved, but they played an important part in a national and then a global process.

A revealing sign of the times is given by two series of BBC radio programs. Toward the end of the war, in 1944, there were talks by leading exponents of three forms of humanism—*Scientific Humanism* (Julian Huxley), *Classical Humanism* (Gilbert Murray), and *Christian Humanism* (J. H. Oldham)—the texts of which were published in *Humanism* (1944). The formation of the humanist movement after the war may be seen as the combination of the first two at the expense of the third. Oldham insisted that humanism depended on theism; Huxley called scientific humanism "a truly religious point of view" and saw it as "the basis for a definite organized religion"; Murray never went so far.

A decade later, in January 1955, Margaret Knight expounded *humanism* in two talks, the broadcasting of which caused widespread controversy and the texts of which were published in *Morals Without Religion* (1955). She called her outlook *scientific humanism*, but far from describing it as a religion she explicitly opposed it to religion. (In both episodes, as was customary, Christian speakers were allowed the last word.)

A powerful negative stimulus to humanism at the end of the war was an authoritative Christian attack on it in the Church of England report *Towards the Conversion of England* (1945), produced by a Commission of Evangelism appointed at the request of the Church Assembly in 1943. This opened with a pessimistic account of "The Situation Before the Church" which emphasized "the wholesale drift from organized religion" during the war, involving a serious decline in religious belief, observance and morality (mainly sexual). It continued with an alarmist analysis of the "underlying causes." The second was said to be "Secular

Education" (despite the Education Act of 1944 which imposed religious education in all State and Church schools); but the first was described as "Humanism the Age-Long Lie," and also "the root sin"! In the old days Christians had attacked infidelity or atheism or secularism or rationalism; now they attacked humanism: "Humanism is the word now commonly used to describe that view of life which sees in man the source of all meaning and value, instead of God." There were sneers at "the humanistic view of life" and "its specious and threadbare creed," and claims that "the record of Humanism is not inspiring," blaming it for capitalism and socialism, dictatorship and war.

The freethought movement responded with glee. Archibald Robertson, a leading ethicist and rationalist (and Marxist), replied in a pamphlet *Anglican Shipwreck* (1945):

> Whatever in the modern world is good, whatever is creative, whatever is hopeful, has its roots in humanism. . . . The humanist position is alone rational and right.

He expanded his arguments in *Man His Own Master* (1949), subtitled "An Essay in Humanism."

Immediately after Margaret Knight's radio broadcasts, humanism was discussed in a special issue of *Twentieth Century* (February 1955). The novelist E. M. Forster contributed a letter, described editorially as being "not exactly a manifesto" but expressing the humanist position. He asked, "How indeed do I define myself?" If he said *atheist*, it was "crude"; if he said *agnostic*, it was "feeble"; if he said *liberal*, it was "impossible":

> If I say I am a humanist there is apt to be a bored withdrawal. On the whole humanist is the best word, though. It expresses more nearly what I feel about myself, and it is Humanism that has been most precisely threatened during the past ten years. Humanism covers my main belief and my main disbelief.

He considered the dogmatic religious and political systems prevailing in the world, and commented, "I assert that there is an alternative in Humanism." But he hoped that there would not so much a campaign for as a celebration of humanism:

> Humanism could better be honored by reciting a list of the things one has enjoyed or found interesting, of the people who have helped one, and of the people whom one has loved and tried to help.

This was widely discussed, frequently reprinted (as a leaflet by the Ethical Union), and strongly criticized—as by C. S. Lewis, in a reply with the bitter title "Lilies That Fester" [Smell Far Worse Than Weeds!], incidentally complaining about the use of *humanism* "since the word has long borne a useful, and wholly different, meaning" (*Twentieth Century*, April 1955).

The main focus for this development was the Ethical movement, and the key factor in this process was the work of Harold Blackham in the Ethical Union. The Union of Ethical Societies became the Ethical Union in 1920, which was incorporated in 1927 with the following official objects:

> To promote by all lawful means the study of ethical principles; to advocate a religion of human fellowship and service, based upon the principle that the supreme aim of religion is the love of goodness, and that moral ideas and the moral life are independent of beliefs as to the ultimate nature of things and a life after death; and, by purely human and natural means, to help men to love, know and do the right in all relations of life.

Blackham joined Stanton Coit at the Ethical Church in 1933 and succeeded him in 1935, and became secretary of the Ethical Union in 1945, but he took a very different view of the task before ethicists and other freethinkers. He was interested neither in preserving nor in reviving nor in criticizing religion, however defined, but in creating and developing and spreading a new concept of humanism, freshly defined, both in Britain and around the world.

Soon before the Second World War began, in September 1938, he had taken part in the conference of the World Union of Freethinkers at Conway Hall in London, which marked the end of the old international freethought movement—and which hardly mentioned humanism. As the war was coming to an end—immediately after the death of Stanton Coit in 1944—he launched the project of establishing a new movement which would provide a synthesis of all constructive forms of humanism and absorb and transcend the existing freethought organizations. And soon after the war ended, he took the initiative in organizing an international conference of the World Union of Freethinkers at Conway Hall, this time specifically on "The Challenge of Humanism" (April 30–May 5, 1946).

Blackham spoke and wrote in every kind of place to every kind of audience in support of his project. He founded and edited the quarterly magazine *The Plain View* (October 1944–May 1965), which was published by the Ethical Union but soon took the subtitle "A Humanist Journal" (April 1947), and which gained the support of both Julian Huxley and Gilbert Murray and also of Bertrand Russell; this was supported by the Ethical Union *News and Notes* (from January 1946), edited by M. L. Burnet.

Blackham and a growing number of colleagues hammered out the principles of their humanism, based on his argument that "scientific humanism must be married to literary humanism" and that "humanists must form themselves into a movement with an adequate social philosophy, a philosophy of civilization" (*Plain View*, July 1946). He also argued that "Rationalists and Liberal Humanists" should "set their hands to the building up of a Third Force between the main developed alternatives of Christianity and Marxism" (*Literary Guide*, December 1948). In a similar way, humanism was later advocated in Ireland (North and South) as a third way between the degenerated alternatives of Catholicism and Protestantism.

Blackham wrote a series of important articles in the *Plain View*. In "What We Mean by Humanism" (February 1950) he said:

It is a decision, a commitment, a faith, a concourse of believers compassed about with a great cloud of witnesses. . . . It is the slow growth of secular self-confidence, freeing itself during centuries from tutelage and authority, nerved by science to break the enchantment of the incomparable classical past and turn to even more dazzling prospects in the open future: it is this secularism, this religion of progress, which has come to be called humanism.

He ended an exposition of "Essentials of Humanism" (August 1954):

Humanism, then, is today an inheritance of great magnitude and magnificence, but in poor repair and in danger of collapse. The first essential is a reconstruction of its basic concepts in the light of what has happened and of new knowledge, *and for the sake of a new initiative in human affairs.* Simply to go back on the ideas and ideals which have made the modern world is a counsel of despair. At any rate, the humanist way is to look at them again informed by what they have led to and by what has been learned since they took shape. And these humanist ideas which are in question are not primarily ideas about the ultimate nature of things; they are central convictions about reason and science, freedom and morality, ideals and values. . . .

Thus, as never before, all that humanism stands for is in question and the world that humanists believe in and want is at stake. Humanist ideas and ideals which have been in the background, part of our total cultural inheritance, unremarked pieces of our mental furniture, are dragged into the centre of critical attention. Shall we throw them out or remodel on them our style of life? That question has never been raised before, and now it is forced on us with the urgency of a world-making decision. *Unless humanists now strive to gain the initiative*, the world will be made by other influences, by ideas and ideals bred in despair or in destructive passions. Thus today humanism is a movement, or else it lacks all seriousness and is nothing. Its call, its demands, its vision can be made good only by the solidarity and effectiveness of a movement. . . .

Humanism is today the commitment to defend, revise, and develop the irreversible ideas and ideals which have made the modern world and are now challenged and threatened. *This commitment is also a recognition and an acceptance of the difficult consequences of these ideas and ideals*, and is therefore a striving to make good the humanist world which is in the making, partly actual, partly ideal. . . .

> Humanism, then, is not a set of opinions, still less the rejection of any set of opinions. It is a body of central conviction about reason and science, freedom and morality, ideals and values, which requires commitment, choice, and action, for it requires the creation of a personal life of one's own and of a world, a humanist civilization. Therefore humanism is a call to all men, a vision of what is to be achieved. [*Original emphasis*]

This was published as the first of a series of Ethical Union pamphlets and leaflets with the general title of "Humanist Thought and Action."

Blackham definitely stated his view in a lecture to the South Place Ethical Society on "What Is Humanism?" (October 2, 1966). He insisted that "Humanism is not a religion, not a philosophy, not a political lobby nor party" (*Monthly Record*, January 1967):

> Essentially, it is an *alternative* to religion, an entirely different way of taking and tackling the world. . . . Humanism, then, as an alternative to religion is a permanent and genuine cause, a programme, a shared vision and activity, a broad social and educational reform movement or party.

Blackham also produced several books. *Living as a Humanist* (1950) was a symposium, whose "purpose is to promote humanism as a fully developed alternative to the historic religions"; "humanism is a permanent tradition in human thinking and living," but "in our day a new movement is called for." *The Human Tradition* (1953) was a scholarly survey of the subject, and *Humanism* (1968) was (at least by intention) a popular introduction to the subject. The latter opened with his final minimum statement of the two basic assumptions of humanism:

> Humanism proceeds from the assumptions *that* man is on his own and this life is all and an assumption *of* responsibility for one's own life and for the life of mankind—an appraisal and an undertaking, two personal decisions.

Blackham was later disappointed by the failure to turn British humanism into a major national movement, but it was he who was mainly responsible for the success of turning it into a movement at all. He also took a leading part in making contact with the growing organizations in other countries and in preparing the ground for an international movement.

Another important figure was Hector Hawton, secretary of the South Place Ethical Society from 1948 to 1954 and then manager of the Rationalist Press Association from 1954 to 1972 and editor of its paper. He argued in "The Future of Humanism" that humanism represented what rationalists and ethicists had in common and that it should also appeal to what he frankly called "fellow-travellers" in religion and politics (*Monthly Record*, October 1950).

He won an American Humanist Association competition with an essay on "Humanism: The Third Way" (again between Christianity and communism), in which he commented: "Humanism is a soul without a body, a stream of ideas without their effective organization" (American *Humanist*, December 1950). He had already said this at an Ethical Union conference (*News and Notes*, October 1950). The truth was rather that humanism was a soul with several bodies—the existing freethought societies—and Blackham and Hawton, along with their colleagues, worked hard to bring them together.

International Humanism

Similar developments were simultaneously taking place in other parts of the world, at the same time and in the same spirit as the foundation of the United Nations Organization and the formulation of the Universal Declaration of Human Rights in the aftermath of the Second World War and the gathering shadow of the cold war.

Here again a crucial figure was Julian Huxley. When he became the first director of the new United Nations Scientific and Cultural Organization (UNESCO) in 1946, he declared himself a scientific humanist—as did John Boyd Orr and G. Brock Chisholm, the first directors respectively of the UN Food and Agriculture Organization and the World Health Organization. Huxley produced a pamphlet, *Unesco: Its Purpose and Its Philosophy*, published in London in September 1946 for the first meeting of the Unesco General Conference in Paris in November 1946. He argued that "Unesco needs not only a set of general aims and objects for itself, but also a working philosophy, a working hypothesis concerning human existence," and he proceeded to explain what he had in mind. He insisted that this could not be "one of the competing theologies of the world" (Islam, Roman Catholicism, Protestant Christianity, Buddhism, Unitarianism, Judaism, Hinduism), or "one of the politico-economic doctrines competing in the world today" ("capitalistic free enterprise, Marxist communism, semi-socialist planning"), or "any special or particular philosophy or outlook" ("existentialism or *élan vital*, rationalism or spiritualism, an economic-determinist or a rigid cyclical theory of human history"), or state worship or class theory, racialism or nationalism, or "an exclusively or primarily other-worldly outlook." No; "its outlook must," he suggested, "be based on some form of humanism"—a "modern humanism," "a world humanism" and "a scientific humanism," indeed "a scientific world humanism, global in extent and evolutionary in background." And he concluded by defining the task of Unesco in the divided postwar world: "That task is to help the emergence of a single world culture." This bold suggestion was not accepted, though after another half-century it seems as cogent and urgent as ever.

The freethought movement had had an international dimension since the formation of the World Union of Freethinkers in 1880, but this was gradually superseded by a new international movement which was specifically humanist. This process was preceded by developments in continental Europe and Asia as well as the United States and Britain.

In the Netherlands after the Second World War there was strong feeling that an alternative was needed both to religious commitment, whether Catholic or Protestant or Jewish, and to political commitment, whether conservative or liberal or socialist—what in the Dutch context were seen as the pillars of society—especially after the extreme confrontation between communism and fascism and the traumatic experience of total war and foreign occupation. Jaap (Joseph Philipp) van Praag, a former Marxist and personalist, took the lead in founding the Humanistisch Verbond (Humanist League) in 1946, separately from the old freethought organizations, and in 1947 he published *Modern humanisme, een renaissance?* (Modern Humanism, a Renaissance?). This action struck a chord, and humanism quickly established itself as a major presence in the Netherlands (a parallel organization was soon founded in Flemish Belgium).

In India there have been major freethought organizations—rationalist, secularist, atheist—at various times in several parts of the country. There had also been a short-lived humanist presence. In 1928 a Humanistic Club was founded in Bangalore by Raja Jai Prithvi Bahadur Singh, author of a three-volume book on *Humanism* (1930); it aimed at "a new interpretation of existing religions, through discovering the common basis of all religions," and published the monthly paper *The Humanist* for four years

A much more ambitious movement was later founded by the Bengali agitator Manavendra Natha Roy (Narendra Nath Bhattacharya), a charismatic leader and prolific writer who played a significant part first in the nationalist movement, then in the Communist International, and again on the Left of the nationalist movement. During the Second World War he opposed both Communists and nationalists, and formed the Radical Democratic Party (RDP) in 1940 and the Indian Federation of Labor in 1941. With the coming of Independence after the war, he turned away from both nationalism and communism—though not from Marxism—toward what he called originally "Renaissance" or "Jacobinism," then "the Humanist tradition," and eventually the "new faith" of *Radical Humanism* or *Integral Humanism.* This was outlined in 1946 in speeches published as *New Orientation* and in the "Twenty-two Theses" of *Principles of Radical Democracy*, and adopted by the RDP; at the same time the Indian Renaissance Institute was formed.

Roy's humanism—sometimes called *Royism*—which combined
social and political radicalism with scientific materialism, provided a
counterpart on the left to the better-known tradition of M. K. Gandhi
and Vinoba Bhave, and influenced the "partyless" socialism of Jaya-
prakash Narayan. In 1947, following independence, Roy's "Humanist
Manifesto" was adopted by the Radical Democratic Party and published as *New Humanism: A Manifesto* (1947). In 1948 the RDP
adopted his statement on the *Practice of New Humanism*, dissolved
itself and became the Radical Humanist Movement (and in 1969 the
Radical Humanist Association); at the same time his English-language
papers *Independent India* (1937) and the *Marxian Way* (1945) became
the *Radical Humanist* and the *Humanist Way* respectively. The radical
humanists continued as an important element in Indian freethought
and politics, and produced several publications, including not only
Roy's own writings but also new writings, such as *Radical Humanism:
The Philosophy of Freedom and Democracy* (1983) by V. M.
Tarkunde, Roy's main successor.

In 1960 the separate Indian Humanist Union was founded by
Narsingh Narain. This was derived from the Society for the Promotion
of Freedom of Thought, founded in 1954, and was less concerned with
politics and more tolerant of religion.

Eventually all these developments converged, given urgency in
the alarming context of the cold war between the capitalist West and
the Communist East, and resulted in the formation of a new international organization. At first several leaders, including Blackham,
hoped that all the sections of the new humanist movement would join
the World Union of Freethinkers, but it soon became clear that this
was not the appropriate arena for international humanism. When the
WUF held another international congress, in Rome in 1949, it decided
that "there could be no weakening of Freethought policy to accom-
modate Humanist Societies"; the latter, disappointed by the slow
progress, decided to make their own way.

In July 1950 the Ethical Union held a special summer school at

Bewdley to discuss the prospects of the new humanism. Harold Blackham set the scene in a series of articles on "Humanist Thought and Action" (*News and Notes*, February–July 1950):

> A humanist movement is not a church, in the sense of a company of believers withdrawn from the world of action with their minds fixed on a hope which transcends the immediate here and now; nor is it a party, in the sense of a body of persons united on a programme of action. It participates in both, however, for it requires of its adherents a self-dedication, and self-discipline, an achieved temper and sentiment, which is a work of withdrawal, reflection, and renewal and requires teaching, understanding, and discussion, and at the same time it is a polemic against other alternatives and a mission to the world, for it claims to be the truth of human life and requires the adherence of all men.

And he brought it down to earth with a bump: "Such a movement cannot exist without visible embodiment, and at the least must have a headquarters, a literature, and periodical conferences."

In the end all the hard work came to flower, if not fruit. In August 1952 an International Congress of Humanism and Ethical Culture was held in Amsterdam, sponsored by the British Ethical Union, the American Humanist Association and the American Ethical Union, the Dutch and Belgian Humanist Leagues, the Indian Radical Humanists, and the Vienna Ethical Society. Julian Huxley presided, and opened with a long speech on "Evolutionary Humanism." He invoked "humanism in the broadest sense, to cover also the rationalist and ethical culture movements, and all others which believe in humanity, and which repudiate supernaturalism on the one hand and state-worship on the other," insisted on "the need to develop humanism as a rival to traditional religions and to secular creeds such as communism," and added that "the humanist movement could exercise some of the functions of a religion in the modern world":

> As I see it, the world is undoubtedly in need of a new religion, and that religion must be founded on humanist principles if it is to meet the new

situation adequately. Humanists have a high task before them, in working out the religious implications of their ideas.

When I say religion I do not mean merely a theology involving belief in a supernatural god or gods; nor do I mean merely a system of ethics, however exalted; nor only scientific knowledge, however extensive; nor just a practical social morality, however admirable and efficient. I mean an organized system of ideas and emotions which relate man to his destiny, beyond and above the practical affairs of every day, transcending the present and existing systems of law and social structure. Such systems of ideas and emotions about human destiny have always existed and will always continue to exist; they certainly include the theistic religions; and I believe we have nothing to lose by using the word *religion* in the broadest possible sense to include non-theistic formulations and systems as well.

He rejected a new synthesis of old religions or anything based on "purely ethical systems" or political ideologies, and called for a new religion:

We must believe that some sort of humanist religion could and should eventually arise, and we must begin studying how it might take shape, and the possibilities for its development.

He argued at length that it should be based on natural and social science, man seen as part of the "evolutionary process" and as the agent of "evolutionary progress." And he concluded:

Man's past includes a primarily religious phase. We now live in a technological (and nationalist) phase. The next phase of history could and in my view should be a humanist phase: let us help towards its emergence.

Some other speakers disagreed about the place of religion and indeed about the meaning of humanism, but they all agreed about the need for an international movement to promote what they called "Ethical and Scientific Humanism," defined as follows:

Dedication to and responsibility for human life by maintenance, furtherance, and development of human values, cultivation of science, loyalty to democratic principles and repudiation of authoritarian principles in all social relations, and practice of good faith, without reliance upon authority or dogma.

The congress expressed its support of UNESCO and endorsed the Universal Declaration of Human Rights and other international conventions, and it concluded by founding the International Humanist and Ethical Union (*Ethical* was inserted on the insistence of the American ethicists). Huxley became president, Blackham became secretary, and Hawton drafted the first international *Declaration on Humanism*:

This Congress is a response to the widespread demand for an alternative to the religions which claim to be based on revelation, on the one hand, and to totalitarian systems, on the other. The alternative offered as a third way out of the present crisis of civilization is Humanism, which is not a new sect, but the outcome of a long tradition that has inspired many of the world's thinkers and creative artists and given rise to science itself. Ethical Humanism unites all those who can no longer believe the various creeds and are willing to base their conviction on respect for man as a spiritual and moral being.

The fundamentals of modern Ethical Humanism are as follows:

1 *It is democratic.* It aims at the fullest development of every human being. It holds that this is a matter of right. The democratic principle can be applied to all human relationships and is not restricted to methods of government.

2 *It seeks to use science creatively, not destructively.* It advocates a world-wide application of scientific method to problems of human welfare. Humanists believe that the tremendous problems with which mankind is faced in this age of transition can be solved. Science gives the means but science does not itself propose ends.

3 *Humanism is ethical. It affirms the dignity of man and the right of the individual to the greatest possible freedom of development compatible with the rights of others.* There is a danger that in seeking to utilize scientific knowledge in a complex society individual freedom may be threatened by the very impersonal machine that has been created to save it. Ethical Humanism, therefore, rejects totalitarian attempts to perfect the machine in order to obtain immediate gains at the cost of human values.

4 *It insists that personal liberty is an end that must be combined with social responsibility in order that it shall not be sacrificed to the improvement of material conditions.* Without intellectual liberty, fundamental research, on which progress must in the long run depend, would not be possible. Humanism ventures to build a world on the free person responsible to society. On behalf of individual freedom Humanism is undogmatic, imposing no creed upon its adherents. It is thus committed to education free from indoctrination.

5 *It is a way of life, aiming at the maximum possible fulfillment through the cultivation of ethical and creative living.* It can be a way of life for everyone everywhere if the individual is capable of the responses required by the changing social order. The primary task of Humanism today is to make men aware in the simplest terms of what it can mean to them and what it commits them to. By utilizing in this context and for purposes of peace the new power which science has given us, Humanists have confidence that the present crisis can be surmounted. Liberated from fear the energies of man will be available for a self-realization to which it is impossible to foresee the limit.

Ethical Humanism is thus a faith that answers the challenge of our times. We call upon all men who share this conviction to associate themselves with us in this cause.

The reference to "fundamentals" raises an intriguing echo of religious fundamentalism; yet there is no mention of religion.

In 1965 the Board of IHEU issued another declaration, *What Ethical Humanism Stands For*:

Ethical Humanism is a complex response to the world of those who hold that man is self-dependent. It rejects absolutes and cannot be characteristically represented by any tabulation of statements. Those that follow should be read as an indication of what humanism stands for, rather than as a declaration of what humanism is.

1 Ethical Humanism expresses a moral conviction; it is acceptance of responsibility for human life in the world.

2 It represents a way of life relying upon human capacities and natural and social resources.

3 Humanist morality starts with an acknowledgement of human interdependence and the need for mutual respect.

4 Ethical Humanism calls for a significant existence made worthwhile through human commitment and acceptance, as a basis for enjoyment and fulfilment.

5 Man becomes human in society; society should provide conditions for the fullest development of each man.

6 Human development requires continuous improvement of the conditions of free inquiry and of an open society.

7 Scientific knowledge progressively established and applied is the most reliable means of improving welfare.

8 Human progress is progress in freedom of choice; human justice is the progressive realization of equality.

9 Justice does not exclude force, but the sole desirable use of force is to suppress the resort to force.

10 Ethical Humanism affirms the unity of man and a common responsibility of all men for all men.

Again, there is no mention of religion. Indeed, despite Huxley's repeated appeals, the members of both old and new humanist organizations around the world showed little and steadily less interest in retaining a religious identity of any kind.

IHEU, based from 1952 to 1995 in Utrecht, was dominated by the original Dutch, American, and British humanist organizations, and later also by the very successful Human-Etisk Forbund (Human-Ethical League) in Norway and the Council for Democratic and Secular Humanism in North America. The World Union of Freethinkers continued to exist, with strong support from France and other Latin countries, and also from Bertrand Russell as one of its presidents, but almost all the various freethought organizations in countries around the world eventually affiliated to IHEU, which became the formal voice of world humanism.

British Humanism II

Back in Britain, the freethought movement slowly but steadily adopted humanism. Freethinkers of all kinds argued about it at Conway Hall and in the *Monthly Record* of the South Place Ethical Society and in the *Literary Guide* of the Rationalist Press Association. Symbolically, when the Conway Discussion Meetings, jointly organized by the two bodies from 1929 to 1939, were revived immediately after the end of the Second World War, the first series in October 1945 concentrated on the question of humanism.

During the war Olaf Stapledon had produced a book, *Beyond the Isms* (1942), arguing that "to-day we are desperately in need of some kind of synthesis of religion and materialism," and insisting on the need for what he called "spirit." In 1946 Olaf Stapledon and Archibald Robertson gave opposing talks at Conway Hall with the title "Is Humanism Enough?" Stapledon's answer was No; he saw humanism as an imperfect attempt at the necessary synthesis, describing it as "an unsatisfactory compromise" because it lacked the necessary religious element (*Monthly Record*, March 1946); Robertson's answer was Yes (*Monthly Record*, June 1946).

But *humanism* was unpopular not just with those who had religious or spiritual tendencies, but also with many old secularists and rationalists who gathered in the National Secular Society (NSS) and the Rationalist Press Association and expressed themselves in the *Freethinker* and the *Literary Guide*. Joseph McCabe's *Rationalist Encyclopaedia* (1948) ignored postwar developments of the term; so did the French *Dictionnaire Rationaliste* (1964). The veteran secularist Chapman Cohen challenged those who called themselves "humanists," echoed Hobson by wondering whether they would be better called "humorists" (though perhaps of "the unconscious variety"), and insisted on a much wider definition of *humanism* (*Freethinker*, January 23, 1944):

Humanism in the sense of acting wisely and kindly to one's fellow is, in however distorted a sense, common to the human race, and beyond that to the higher animal world. . . . To some extent every human being is a humanist. . . . We see no objection to the term *humanist* being applied to everybody from dustman to duke and from fool to philosopher.

The veteran rationalist, Adam Gowans Whyte, similarly said in *The Story of the RPA* (1949): "*Humanism*, which is still used occasionally as a mild synonym for Rationalism, suffers from vagueness which permits too wide a variety of interpretations." The veteran secularist and rationalist H. Cutner said, "I cannot say that I am particularly enamored of this word *Humanism* which now appears to be co-opted by anybody and everybody" (*Freethinker*, December 7, 1952). A. E. Heath, president of the RPA, said in his *Rationalist Review* column, "I am not entirely happy about the current fashion of substituting the word *humanism* for *rationalism*" (*Literary Guide*, October 1955), and again, "I am still, unrepentantly, of the opinion that Humanism, in spite of or because of its great historical connotations, is not really a happy term" (January 1956). G. J. Henry Lloyd, former secretary of the Humanist Council, worried about confusion over the term *humanism* and the connection with religion in "The Semantic Problem in the Rationalist and Humanist Movements" (*University Libertarian*, Winter 1958). E. Royston Pike, speaking at Conway Hall on "Scientific Humanism: A Critical View" (*Monthly Record*, July 1958), drew an unfavorable caricature:

Humanism is the name which seems to be increasingly favored for the omnibus in which Rationalists, Ethicists, Secularists, Atheists, Agnostics, Freethinkers, and indeed the whole tribe of unbelievers are being taken for a ride. . . .

One objection to *humanism* was that it tried to be all things to all men, and ended by being nothing to any; another was that it was simply a euphemism for unbelief which fooled neither believers nor unbelievers; yet another, that it was little more than a Christian heresy, was often put by Christian opponents; even another, that it was the work of a fifth column within the freethought movement, was seriously advanced by some activists in the mid-1960s (Two of the most paranoid protagonists of this popish plot later themselves became Roman Catholics!).

Even supporters of the word were often uncertain about it. Henry Tompkins, a leading positivist, said he preferred *humanitist* but accepted *humanist*, commenting: "We shall, I suppose, have to be content with this name despite its amorphous meaning and give it new meaning" (*Monthly Record*, February 1954). An anonymous writer commented: "I dislike the word, for are we not all human beings? But what better word can we use in its place?" (*Monthly Record*, April 1958). Hawton commented at one point that "the logical way out would be to invent a new name altogether" (*Humanist*, December 1961), but admitted at another that "the word has come to stay, whether we like it or not" (*Humanist*, May 1961). And Barbara Smoker repeated editorially that "the label *Humanist* has stuck whether we like it or not" (*Ethical Record*, June 1966).

J. B. Coates suggested another kind of alternative in an English version of Mounier's *Personalism*. He doubted whether *humanism* was a sufficient ideology (*Rationalist Annual*, 1953), and offered "A Personalist Analysis of the Crisis" (*Plain View*, May 1952), involving the absorption into personalism of the best of Christianity and Marxism as well as humanism. But he later expounded plain humanism in his book *A Challenge to Christianity* (1958), with "A Humanist Manifesto" in an appendix.

Julian Huxley's insistence that humanism was or should be a religion was complicated by the influence on him of Teilhard de Chardin. When Huxley edited a symposium of distinguished contributors, *The Humanist Frame* (1961), introducing it with a further call for "Evolutionary Humanism," there was growing criticism of his religiosity. Huxley's last collection of occasional writings was *Essays of a Humanist* (1964), including the introduction to *The Humanist Frame*.

And in the final edition of *Religion Without Revelation* (1967), he still called for a "new and permanent natural religion," "an evolutionary and humanist religion," and again for "transhumanism," raising humanity to a higher "psychosocial" stage of evolution.

Few other humanists followed this line, though there were continual suggestions that humanism was or should become some kind of religion or faith, and there were shifts of opinion. Barbara Smoker spoke for many. For a time she defended humanism as a form of "natural religion" based on "spiritual communion" (*Monthly Record*, May 1956, and *News and Notes*, November 1958); but as editor of the *Monthly Record* and *Ethical Record* (1964–1970) she no longer supported this view; then in her educational booklet *Humanism* (1973) she decided that humanism was not a religion; and as president of the National Secular Society (1971–1996) she rejected not only religion but such words as *spiritual* and *communion*.

S. G. Jacobi spoke for a few, warning that on its own scientific humanism could turn into "scientific inhumanism," and arguing that humanism must provide "A Faith for Modern Man" (*Literary Guide*, April 1958):

> There is a supreme need today for a new form of religion or faith—call it what you will—shorn of the shibboleths and dogmas of orthodox religion, in tune with the latest scientific discoveries about man and the universe, and yet fulfilling man's deepest needs of communion with others, contemplation, and a consciousness of those ethical principles that will enable him to live, a fully integrated human being, in harmony with his fellows.

Such views tended to attract some verbal but little practical support, and also much criticism. Ronald W. Hepburn's contribution to the symposium *Objections to Humanism* (1963) questioned what he called the "Humanist Theology" of Dewey and Huxley and their followers. And most secular and scientific humanists found religious talk embarrassing or irritating.

The term *humanism* itself continued to cause trouble. Some people joked about it, others complained about it. Kathleen Nott frequently remarked in 1964 that the common conception of a humanist was "someone who was rude to God or else someone who was kind to animals." R. Smith repeated that "it isn't *Humanists* they should be called, but *Humorists*" (*Freethinker*, December 8, 1967). Benjamin Farrington rejected such terms as *scientific* or *evolutionary* or any other humanism, and insisted: "I like my Humanism plain. . . . The simple word *Humanism* best conveys its two aspects of comprehensiveness and brotherliness" (*Rationalist Annual*, 1965). Peter Crommelin repeated the old objection: "There are as many humanisms as there are human individuals" (*Freethinker*, January 19, 1968).

The secularist David Tribe commented in *100 Years of Freethought* (1967) that "the word which now enjoys the greatest vogue in freethought circles, *humanism*, is the vaguest term of all," though he admitted that "it has proved very serviceable." And he added in *Nucleoethics* (1972): "The fact that so many people of widely differing world-views can lay claim to humanism reflects a complex history and an inherent vagueness."

But the growing movement favored the word, more people defended it, sometimes offering personal versions of "A Humanist Manifesto"—such as Harold Blackham (*Monthly Record*, February 1951) and David Tribe himself (*Monthly Record*, July 1959). There was wide approval of *scientific humanism*, as expounded in the radio talks by Margaret Knight which gave it such wide publicity, or by Antony Flew, who summarized his position as follows: "scientific primarily as regards matters of fact; humanist concerning questions of value" (*Literary Guide*, August 1955). Alex Comfort had actually advocated scientific humanism on the radio six years earlier, in a series of talks published as *The Pattern of the Future* (1949), which aroused strong support as well as strong opposition. Other influential exponents included C. D. Darlington and C. H. Waddington, J. D. Bernal and J. Bronowski, Fred Hoyle and Hermann Bondi.

In the end *humanism* became the generic term for the whole freethought movement. There was editorial discussion in the *Monthly Record* of the "older humanism" which had marked the secularist, rationalist, and ethical movement and the "new humanism" which was superseding it (February 1960). Secular, rationalist, and ethical societies became humanist societies (starting in Manchester in 1948), with the exceptions of the South Place Ethical Society and the Leicester Secular Society (the only ones which owned their own premises). A Humanist Council was formed in 1950, on Hawton's initiative, to coordinate first the Rationalist and Ethical and later also the Secularist and Positivist organizations, was superseded by an abortive Humanist Association in 1957, and was reconstituted in 1959. A University Humanist Federation was formed in 1959 to coordinate the student societies. Humanist Group Action was formed in 1961 to organize practical work

The Ethical Union considered changing its name to the Humanist Union in 1959 and to the British Humanist Association (BHA) in 1962, and the Rationalist Press Association considered changing its name to the Humanist and Rationalist Association in 1961. Instead, however, the two organizations worked together, and in May 1963 they jointly formed a new British Humanist Association as an umbrella organization, with Huxley as president and Blackham as director. It was launched at the House of Commons in May 1963, Huxley continuing to emphasize the religious dimension and insisting that "Humanism is the only system of beliefs which could unite all races of mankind." A year later this step was hailed with pardonable exaggeration in *Humanist News* as "an event which can be said to signal the formation of the Humanist Movement in this country" (May/June 1964). It was accompanied by the publication in 1963 of a plain woman's and a plain man's guide to that movement—*What Humanism Is About* by Kit Mouat (Jean Mackay), and *The Humanist Revolution* by Hector Hawton.

The RPA was forced for technical reasons to withdraw from the BHA in 1966, and the Ethical Union accordingly adopted the new name and absorbed the new organization in 1967, with the following formal objects:

1 To advocate a responsible self-governing way of life which is of service to the community.
2 To promote knowledge of the psychological and social foundation of
  morality as an essential factor in the advance of civilization.
3 To give practical service to the community as an example of and in
  pursuance of the preceding objects.

In June 1965 the BHA adopted as its symbol Denis Barrington's
"Happy Man" (later politically corrected to the "Happy Human"),
which was soon adopted by other humanist organizations in Britain
and then around the world. The BHA sponsored various specialist organizations—Humanist Housing Association, Humanist Holidays,
Humanist Teachers Association, and so on—and issued a General
Statement of Policy in July 1967, and it became the largest freethought
organization in the country.

In June 1967 the BHA established the Humanist Trust as a charitable subsidiary, for "the advancement of the education of the public
. . . with respect to the ideas and principles known as Humanism, that
is to say, the moral and social development of the community free
from theistic or dogmatic beliefs and doctrine." In 1983 this legally
acceptable definition of humanism was adopted by the BHA, which
thus acquired charitable status (following the success of the South
Place Ethical Society in 1980) with the following objects:

1 The mental and moral improvement of the human race by means of
  the advancement of Humanism, that is to say, the moral and social
  development of the community free from theistic or dogmatic beliefs
  and doctrines.
2 The advancement of education and in particular the study of
  Humanism and the dissemination of knowledge of its principles.

Even when freethought organizations retained their titles they
adjusted their nomenclature—the Ethical Union had changed its *News
and Notes* to *Humanist News* in April 1964; the RPA changed the
name of its journal *The Literary Guide* to *The Humanist* in October

1956, and published as *Reason in Action* (1956) a symposium of essays on humanism; South Place adopted "Ethical Humanism" as its informal object in 1961, and named Conway Hall a "Humanist Centre" in May 1964; the *Freethinker* was subtitled as "Freethought and Humanism Weekly" from January 1966, "Humanist World [*sic*] Weekly" from November 1967, and "Secular Humanist Weekly" from August 1970.

A significant factor was the acceptance of the shift to humanism by Bertrand Russell, the leading English-speaking philosopher in the twentieth century, and a strong supporter of the NSS and the RPA. He was hostile to Pragmatism before the First World War, and wary of scientific humanism before the Second World War. In 1951 he mischievously told Warren Allen Smith that he was reluctant to accept *humanism*, because "I think, on the whole, that the non-human part of the cosmos is much more interesting and satisfactory than the human part" (American *Humanist*, October 1951). But he welcomed the change of name by the *Literary Guide*, and in 1967 contributed to a symposium on *Socialist Humanism*.

Similarly, Albert Einstein, the leading scientist in the twentieth century, called his last book *Essays in Humanism* (1950), and Karl Popper, the leading philosopher of science in the twentieth century, wrote an essay on "Humanism and Reason" (1952), included in *Conjectures and Refutations* (1963).

Religious or Secular Humanism?

Although many if not most of the individuals and organizations in this long process were nonreligious or antireligious, many were still religious.

The American humanists were almost all religious to begin with, and the *Humanist Manifesto* of 1933 discussed humanism entirely as a religious ideology, explicitly as "religious humanism." Edwin H. Wilson, the Unitarian minister who ran the American Humanist Association and edited *The Humanist* for several years, in 1963 founded the Fellowship of Religious Humanists, which published the magazine *Religious Humanism* from 1967, and still exists as the Friends of Religious Humanism. Lloyd and Mary Morain's book *Humanism as the Next Step* (1954), subtitled "An Introduction for Liberal Protestants, Catholics, and Jews," introduced humanism as "The Fourth Faith," both a religion and a philosophy. The American *Humanist Manifesto* of 1973 still admitted religious humanism. Many of the American Unitarian and Universalist congregations which merged into the Unitarian Universalist Association in 1961 see themselves as both humanist and religious, as do many Unitarians in Britain and other countries. The Free Religious Congregations in Germany (*Freie Religiöse Gemeinde*), which were formed in the mid-nineteenth century and survived into the later twentieth century, took the same view.

Similarly the later progressive elements in the Christian churches in Britain who have been abandoning theism and joining in the Sea of Faith movement call their position *Christian humanism*, and the progressive Jews in both America and Britain and also in Israel who have been abandoning theism call their position *humanistic Judaism*. It is wrong to call these positions "contradictions in terms" or to call their adherents hypocrites. There is an infinitely wide spectrum extending from total belief to total unbelief, and the intermediate points have often employed combinations of terms. After all, even those who most strongly insist on our sense of humanism in the present would hardly deny the name of *humanist* to such figures of the past as Erasmus or Montaigne, Voltaire or Paine.

For a long time, most American humanists were determined to establish that their humanism *was* religious. One theoretical motive was that they were reluctant to abandon the psychological and sociological support of their religious background, and one practical motive was to gain acceptance for humanists as conscientious objectors to military service on the same basis as religious objectors, and in other such legal predicaments; indeed the U.S. Supreme Court went some way toward recognizing ethical culture and secular humanism as forms of religion (*Torcaso* v. *Watkins*, 1961).

After a time, however, most American humanists were determined to establish that their humanism was *not* religious, that it was rather an alternative to or substitute for or rejection of religion. This time one theoretical motive was that they had now moved so far from whatever religious backgrounds they had that they no longer wished to be identified with them, and one practical motive was to gain acceptance for such "humanistic" doctrines as biological evolution in public schools, where religious teaching or observance is constitutionally excluded. At the same time American humanists took a leading part in the growing "skeptical" movement which turned the critique of the claims of supernatural religion to a critique of claims of paranormal phenomena, which generalized their opposition to all forms of superstition.

During the 1960s and 1970s the phrase *secular humanism* was gradually adopted as the description of many American humanists; though they sometimes accepted the description of a *quasi-religion*— still *religious* but not a *religion*, following Dewey. *Secular humanism* was also employed by several British humanists in a rather different sense, intending to dissociate themselves from religious tendencies in the new humanist movement and to associate themselves with the secularist tradition of the old freethought movement.

This situation was finally confirmed in the United States by the publication of *A Secular Humanist Declaration* (in the first issue of *Free Inquiry*, Winter 1980/1981), and the subsequent formation of the Council for Democratic and Secular Humanism (CODESH)—shortened in 1995 to the Council for Secular Humanism (*Democratic*, which had been used to distinguish Western humanism from Russian communism, was no longer necessary after the collapse of the Soviet Union).

The *Secular Humanist Declaration* was drafted by Paul Kurtz and signed by hundreds of humanists all over the world. It contained ten long theses, but it still avoided any clear definitions, mentioning only that "Secular humanists may be agnostics, atheists, rationalists or skeptics." It also avoided the actual rejection of religion, including statements on one side that "we are generally skeptical about supernatural claims" and that "we are doubtful of traditional views of God and divinity" and on the other side that "we recognize the importance of religious experience."

Nowadays humanism is generally seen as definitely separate from and indeed hostile to religion. However, Harry Stopes-Roe has proposed and many humanists have agreed that humanism is a "stance for living" or "life stance," which is claimed to be somehow "analogous" with religion in a philosophical and psychological sense, and which has also proved to be useful in legal and educational contexts.

And, finally, a secular humanist is no longer a classical scholar. Most people who call themselves humanists today, like Shakespeare, have small Latin, and less Greek, and few of them are scholars or intellectuals of any kind. They are simply a growing number of people of all kinds, who try to do as they would be done by and to make the best of their life together without any invisible means of support.

Other Humanisms

The word *humanism* has of course continued to be used with other meanings than those adopted by the humanist movement. The senses of Renaissance humanism, and of classical humanism beforehand or of Enlightenment humanism afterward, are the main historical meanings of the word. The educational sense still exists, and most academic institutions have departments or faculties of humanities whose members are sometimes called humanists and whose activities are sometimes called humanism. There are still religious as well as nonreligious or antireligious humanists. But several other quite distinct senses have also been used.

Socialist Humanism and Antihumanism

Marx's early conception of humanism, as the philosophical aspect of the political ideology of communism, gained new strength when

Marxist parties took power in several countries, from Russia at the end of the First World War to most of Eastern Europe at the end of the Second World War.

In some Communist countries *humanism*—*gumanizm* in Russia, *humanismus* in several satellites—was used for the ideal of public morality and in particular for the moral education given in schools in place of religious education. Humanism was discussed from the Marxist point of view in many articles and several books; one of the latter was translated into English—Maria Petrosyan's *Humanism* (1972). In October 1961, the Communist party of the Soviet Union included in *The Road to Communism* a formal Moral Code, among whose ideals was "a spirit of collectivism, industry and humanism." This was greeted with cynicism and even sarcasm by several Western humanists.

Between the world wars, Antonio Gramsci, Karl Korsch, and György Lukács emphasized the humanist aspects of their unorthodox versions of Marxism. After the Second World War, Raya Dunayevskaya emphasized the humanism of Marx, in *Marxism and Freedom* (1958) and several other books, and insisted that a Marxism free from the distortions of Stalinism, Trotskyism, and Maoism would be "a new humanism." In France, Henri Lefebvre and Roger Garaudy followed a similar line. In Germany and the United States, the members of the Frankfurt School often stressed the humanist aspects of their moderate Marxism.

In the United States, Erich Fromm tried to combine Marx and Freud, bringing together the "humanistic ethics" of *Man For Himself* (1947) and the "humanistic psychoanalysis" of *The Sane Society* (1955) into a synthesis of humanistic socialism. Fromm edited the impressive symposium on *Socialist Humanism* (1965), defining humanism as, "in simplest terms, the belief in the unity of the human race and man's potential to perfect himself by human efforts," and including dozens of contributors from Western and Eastern Europe and North America, mostly moderate Marxists but also such free spirits as Danilo Dolci and Bertrand Russell. And Ken Coates later edited an inferior symposium of *Essays on Socialist Humanism* (1972).

Among the socialists involved in the so-called New Left after the Second World War, *humanism* was used to describe the more humane and democratic variety of Western Marxism. Thus during the late 1950s such British intellectuals as Edward Thompson and Stuart Hall respectively edited the *New Reasoner* and *Universities and Left Review*, both subtitled as journals of "Socialist Humanism."

Humanism was also affirmed by some of the dissident intellectuals in Communist countries, either within or against Marxism, especially the so-called revisionists of Eastern Europe. It was criticized as mere "abstract humanism," but the trouble was that in the climate of those places at that time it was all too concrete. In Yugoslavia, Milovan Djilas and Vladimir Dedijer called themselves humanists; so did the Praxis group of philosophers, who were openly active from the mid-1960s to the mid-1970s (Mihailo Marković published books on socialist humanism in both Yugoslavia and Britain, and became active in the International Humanist and Ethical Union, but later became an apologist for Serbian nationalism). In Czechoslovakia, Karel Kosík and Ivan Sviták called themselves humanists. So did Athanase Joja in Romania, and some members of the Budapest School in Hungary. In Poland, Leszek Kołakowski wrote about Marxist humanism before he later abandoned both Marxism and humanism.

In Russia itself, one of the most important dissidents, the scientist Andrei Sakharov, called himself a humanist as well as a Marxist; he was deported, but saw the fall of the Communist regime before his death. By contrast, the young poet Yuri Galanskov rejected Marxism and turned to nonpolitical or even antipolitical humanism, contributing a remarkable *Human Manifesto* (*Chelovecheski Manifest*) to the first issue of his samizdat paper *Phoenix* (1961); he was arrested and detained in a psychiatric hospital in 1961, arrested again in 1967 and imprisoned in a labor camp, where he died in 1972.

On the other hand some Marxists turned against humanism—either Stalinists and Maoists who preferred "proletarian" Socialism to what they described as "liberal" or "bourgeois" or even "petty-bourgeois" humanism, or Western intellectuals who were attracted by the changing fashions of structuralism, poststructuralism, deconstructionism, and postmodernism in general. The French Communist leader Louis Althusser (who later strangled his wife) included in *Pour Marx* (1965)—translated as *For Marx* (1969)—a 1963 essay on "Marxism and Humanism," trying to dissociate the two. Edward Thompson wrote a furious reply. Humanism was condemned as obsolete and prescientific by postmodernists like Michel Foucault and Jacques Derrida. It has also been considered as sexist and patriarchal by some feminists, and racist and imperialistic by some socialists. Contemporary arguments for and against humanism were covered by Kate Soper's *Humanism and Anti-Humanism* (1986) and Tony Davies's *Humanism* (1997).

But the older tradition, embodied by Léon Blum in France before the Second World War, calling for "Socialism on a human scale," and by Alexander Dubcek in Czechoslovakia in 1968, calling for "Socialism with a human face," is probably the strongest stream on the moderate Left. It has inspired many if not most followers of left-wing movements and parties, and during the twentieth century it has increasingly been called *humanism*.

Humanism has been an essential element of collectivist or communist anarchism (following Bakunin rather than Proudhon), though not always of individualist anarchism (following Max Stirner). The ideology of the libertarian situationists in the 1960s has been called *cultural humanism*. And the utopian theory of Marshall McLuhan about the mass media, which has been called *digital humanism*, has been put into practice on the Internet.

Fascism and Humanism

At the other end of the political spectrum, Benito Mussolini, a free-thinking socialist before he became a Fascist dictator, proclaimed that the regime he established in Italy in 1922 was "a new humanism";

some intellectual supporters of Adolf Hitler invoked the "new humanism" or "third humanism" of German cultural history, matching the Nazi "Third Empire"; the right-wing French elements which ran the Vichy regime from 1940 claimed that it embodied "ethical humanism"; and Philippe Lacoue-Labarthe in *La Fiction du politique* (1987)—translated as *The Fiction of the Political* (1990)—agreed that in some sense "Nazism is a humanism"!

Ecology

There have been contradictory views of humanism in the Green or ecology movement. The social ecology tendency, led by Murray Bookchin, has insisted on humanism; the deep ecology tendency, led by Arne Naess, has denounced humanism; the political ecology tendency has tried to transcend humanism and proclaimed *posthumanism*. David Ehrenfeld attacked *The Arrogance of Humanism* (1978); Henryk Skolimowski argued for a mystical *Ecological Humanism* (1976); and Peter Cadogan, when he was secretary of the South Place Ethical Society (1970–1980), argued for a mysterious *apocalyptic humanism.*

Existentialism

Conceptions of humanism sometimes appeared in existentialism, the philosophical movement based on the doctrine that man makes his own nature, part of which is freedom of choice (and in the allied movement of phenomenology). The early exponents of existentialism were mainly religious, from Søren Kierkegaard (who detested philosophy as "the purely human view of the world—the *humane* standpoint," and dismissed humanism as "vaporized Christianity"), but several later ones were nonreligious or even antireligious, and some approached humanism.

The French philosopher Jean Paul Sartre, arguing against Catholic humanists on one side and Communist humanists on the other, and also against any religion of humanity and any kind of "bourgeois" humanism, insisted in a lecture that *Existentialism Is a Humanism* (1946), because it is based on man making himself; the German philosopher Martin Heidegger replied in his *Letter on Humanism* (1947), disagreeing about both existentialism and humanism. (Spice is added to their dispute by the facts that Heidegger had been a fellow-traveller with the Nazis and Sartre was to be a fellow-traveller with the Communists; the latter later called his position *Revolutionary* or *Dialectical Humanism*.)

Maurice Merleau-Ponty wrote *Humanism and Terror* (1947), discussing the possibility of a nonterroristic humanistic society in the light of the experience of Communist dictatorship; and Karl Jaspers included in *Existentialism and Humanism* (1952) a discussion of the "Premises and Possibilities of a New Humanism." But most humanists and most existentialists have alike doubted whether existentialism is really a humanism.

Humanistic Psychology

An explicitly humanist phenomenon is the school of so-called humanistic psychology, which originated in the United States during the 1960s, and which plays up rather than down the emotional and spontaneous aspects of human personality and concentrates on group activity and "peak experiences," and leans toward existentialist and oriental philosophy. The main figures were Carl Rogers and Abraham Maslow in the United States and were R. D. Laing and John Rowan in Britain. Similar traditions are the individual psychology of Alfred Adler, a form of psychoanalysis which concentrated on personal and social factors, the Gestalt Psychology of Wolfgang Köhler and Gestalt Psychotherapy of Frederick Perls, and the rational-emotive therapy of

Albert Ellis. There is also a movement of humanistic sociology in the United States.

Behaviorism

Another relation is behaviorism, the school founded by the American psychologist J. B. Watson, expressed in his book *Behaviorism* (1925), which plays down the concept of the introspective mind and plays up the external behavior of organisms. This might seem alien to humanism, but such leading behaviorists as B. F. Skinner in the United States and H. J. Eysenck in Britain were actively involved in the humanist movement.

Objectivism

A more unlikely candidate for humanist affiliation is the so-called objectivism of the Russian-American thinker Ayn Rand (Alisa Rosenbaum). It is certainly strongly rationalist and atheist, but at the same time so individualist and elitist that it seems far from humanism as understood by most humanists.

Scientology

An even more unlikely candidate is Scientology, the quasi-religious psychiatric cult founded by L. Ron Hubbard as Dianetics in 1950; yet from time to time from the 1950s to the 1970s some Scientologists claimed to be humanists, partly because they rejected a personal God and partly because they adopted pseudoscientific terminology.

Superhumanism, Transhumanism, Posthumanism

During the late nineteenth century, Friedrich Nietzsche had advocated what was sometimes called *superhumanism*; during the early twentieth century, Julian Huxley advocated what he called *transhumanism*.

During the late twentieth century, both terms were revived by American groups on the West Coast advocating various forms of *superhumanism* and *transhumanism*. The latter is defined by so-called Extropians (who defy entropy) as "philosophies of life that seek the continuation and acceleration of the evolution of intelligent life beyond its currently human form and limits by means of science and technology, guided by life-promoting principles and values, while avoiding religion and dogma."

Their goal is *posthumanism*, meaning the state of being "posthuman," for "persons of unprecedented physical, intellectual, and psychological ability, self-programming and self-defining, potentially immortal, unlimited individuals," who (or which) "have overcome the biological, neurological, and psychological constraints evolved into humans," through the use of such techniques as "genetic engineering, neural-computer integration, molecular nanotechnology, and cognitive science."

Some have even adopted a new form of *superhumanism*, based on the transcendence of human beings by superhuman computers or robots.

African Humanism

Back in the real world, during the anticolonialist struggle after the Second World War, humanism was invoked by several African leaders, especially those involved with left-wing intellectual circles in France.

The French West Indian writer Frantz Fanon included in his influential book, *Les Damnés de la terre* (1961)—translated as *The Damned* (1963) and *The Wretched of the Earth* (1964)—a lecture to the Congress of Black Artists and Writers in Rome 1959, insisting that nations and races must be transcended and nationalism and racialism must be replaced, that "this new humanity . . . cannot do otherwise than to define a new humanism."

Léopold Sédar Senghor, the poet and first president of Senegal in 1960, who popularized the cultural concept of *Négritude*, included "the philosophy of humanism" in his book *On African Socialism* (1959), later wrote a book called *Négritude et Humanisme* (1964), and in his contribution to Fromm's *Socialist Humanism* equated *Négritude* and *socialism* with *humanism*. Ahmed Sékou Touré, the founding president of Guinea in 1958, also mentioned "a new humanism" during the 1950s. And Kwame Nkrumah, the founding president of Ghana in 1960, advocated a form of African humanism which he called *consciencism* (1964).

In Haiti, *humanism* was proclaimed alongside *Négritude* and *socialism* by dissident black intellectuals like Jacques Roumain and René Depestre.

Above all, when the British colony of Northern Rhodesia became the independent state of Zambia in 1964, its founding president Kenneth Kaunda proposed that *humanism* should become the national philosophy. This was unanimously accepted in April 1967 by the National Council and in August 1967 by the Annual Conference of the ruling United National Independence Party. *Zambian humanism* was used to describe the eclectic and syncretic acceptance of all religious as well as nonreligious beliefs in the postcolonialist regime (including the public display of posters with the slogan *Be Humanist!*). In theory it combined the best of European and African social morality; in practice it acted as an ideological cloak for this particular one-party dictatorship, which fell in 1992.

How sad that the first country to adopt *humanism* as its official ideology should do so in such a way, and that most of the other forms of *African humanism* betrayed the basic principles of humanism.

Homaranism, Humanitism, Humanitarism

There have also been occasional variations not so much of the idea as on the word *humanism*.

The Polish doctor Ludwik Lazar Zamenhof, who invented the "neutral language" Esperanto in 1878, was much more interested in founding a "neutral religion"; he hoped that the former would be employed and the latter would be adopted by a "neutral people," who would work to end the divisions in humanity. The first Esperantist hymn ended: "All humanity must be united into one family." When he began preaching his religion in 1901 he called his new faith *Hillelismo*, after the first-century rabbi. In 1906 he published the *Dogmas of Hillelism*, which began: "I am human, and the only ideals that exist for me are purely human." But *Hillelism* sounded too narrowly Jewish, so from 1906 he called it *homaranismo*, the Esperanto equivalent of *humanism*.

Homaranism became known as his "inner idea," and he increasingly concentrated on it. In 1912 he actually resigned from the leadership of the Esperantist movement to develop it. In 1913 he published a revised *Declaration on Homaranism*, which began: "I am a human being, and I regard the whole of humanity as one family." He intended to launch Homaranism as a world faith at a congress in Bern in August 1914; but this was prevented by the beginning of the First World War, and he died before its end. (Most of his family died in the Holocaust during the Second World War.) Homaranism was influenced by positivism and Baha'i (Zamenhof's daughter joined the latter), resembled ethicism, and anticipated the religious humanism of American Unitarians and Julian Huxley; but it was too individual and idealistic for its time.

The Czech philosopher and politician Tomás Masaryk, who was the first president of Czechoslovakia after the First World War, adopted the term *humanitism* as distinct from tender-minded humanitarianism and tough-minded humanism (was it relevant that his wife was an American Unitarian?). His lectures of 1898 which were published as *Idéaly humanitní* (1901)—translated first as *Ideals of Humanity* (1938) and then as *Humanistic Ideals* (1971)—examined various political and philosophical ideologies and chose democratic liberalism and moderate nationalism (not far from the ideals of Václav Havel, who was the first president of Czechoslovakia after the collapse of Communism seventy years later).

The Romanian writer Eugen Relgis adopted *humanitarism*, a highly abstract and romantic version of humanism which had some influence in Latin America. His pamphlet *Principiile umanitariste* (1922)—translated first as *What Is Humanitarism?* (1966) and then as *Principles of Humanism* (1974)—proclaimed the need both to "deify Man" and to "humanize Man."

Siloism

During the 1960s the Argentinian thinker "Silo" (Mario Luis Rodríguez Cobos) developed an idiosyncratic mystical psychology, and during the 1970s this became the basis of a mysterious international cult which took several forms and several names. During the 1980s it adopted *humanism*, appearing variously as the "Humanist Party," the "Humanist Forum," "Humanist Clubs," and the "Humanist Movement" (and also as several "Green" organizations). In January 1989 a conference in Florence issued a *Declaration of Humanist Principles* and formed a "First [*sic*] Humanist International," and in October 1993 a conference in Moscow formed a "World Center for Humanist Studies." Silo issued a definitive *Document of the Humanist Movement* in May 1993.

His ideology, which is sometimes called *new humanism* or *universalist humanism*, or just *Siloism*, is based on general humanistic principles, with a strong social and political bias toward the left and with special opposition to exploitation and violence, and it has attracted many young people from time to time in some places. It may perhaps be forgiven its rather absurd theories and rather sinister practices, as well as its rather confusing nomenclature, for the sake of its admirably brief and clear statement of fundamental humanist principle:

Nothing above the human, and no human above another.

World Humanism

And finally, or perhaps firstly, there is the most fundamental humanism of all—from the original theory of the Greek Stoics and Epicureans more than two thousand years ago, which taught that all men (and women) are brothers (and sisters), to the ultimate theory of the modern age, which is embodied, or at least approached, by the vulgar humanism of world politics.

A series of national statements and international agreements has developed a structure of recognized human rights—the *Declaration of Independence* of 1776 and the Constitution of the United States of America of 1787; the official versions of the *Declaration of the Rights of Man and the Citizen* adopted during the French Revolution by the National Assembly in 1789 and the Convention in 1793, and the unofficial *Declaration of the Rights of Woman and the Citizeness* written by Olympe de Gouges (Marie Gouze) in September 1791 (she was guillotined in the Terror, partly for her feminism, in November 1793); the various Geneva Conventions from 1864 onward and Hague Conventions from 1899 onward; the Covenant of the League of Nations in 1920 and the Charter of the United Nations Organization in 1945; the Universal Declaration of Human Rights in 1948, and the subsequent regional and sectional declarations and conventions: the whole monitored by international aid and relief agencies, from the Red Cross in 1863 onward, and by human rights organizations from Amnesty International in 1961 onward, reported by the independent media, and ultimately subject to the public opinion of a notional world community.

In theory, all these together amount to a cumulative and accumulating documentation of a world humanism based on universal human values, assuming the equality of all human beings and the unity of the whole human species. As Winwood Reade said in *The Martyrdom of Man* (1872), "There is only One Man upon the earth." In practice, however, one might well say of this humanism what Gandhi said when he was asked what he thought of Western civilization: "It would be a good idea!"

A cautionary tale may be found in Cuba. When Fidel Castro took power at the beginning of 1959, he proclaimed that the new regime was neither capitalist nor Communist, that it opposed all forms of totalitarianism, whether of the Right, which gave liberty without bread, or of the Left, which gave bread without liberty, and that its ideology was "liberty with bread, without terror—that is, *humanism*." Cuba might have become the first officially humanist country; but in 1961, squeezed between the capitalist West and the Communist East, the regime adopted socialism, and the people got little bread, less liberty, and much terror.

If humanity is to survive, some form of humanism is its best last chance. As Bertrand Russell said, first in his radio talk on "Man's Peril from the Hydrogen Bomb" (December 1954), and then in the manifesto of the Committee of 100, "Act or Perish" (October 1960):

Remember your humanity, and forget the rest.

Conclusion

The words *humanism* and *humanist* continue to have many meanings. Even the sense used by the formal humanist movement is not always clear and distinct. There are still old arguments whether humanism is a religion or a philosophy, a "life-stance" analogous with religion or a worldview opposed to religion, a way of life or an evasion of responsibility, a movement or an attitude. There are also new arguments whether it is in danger of concentrating on human beings at the expense of other living things (expressed in the new term *species-ism*) or of concentrating on human interests at the expense of the environment (opposed by the new versions of *ecology*). There are occasional arguments whether *humanism* is the best word after all, questions about reverting to old words such as *atheism* or *secularism* or *rationalism*, and even proposals for adopting new words—such as *eupraxophy*, suggested by Paul Kurtz (*Free Inquiry*, Winter 1987).

Nevertheless, our version of *humanism* does have a definite meaning, even if we have difficulty agreeing on its definition. And of course our system of thought is much older than the word we now use to describe it. The tradition of humanism in our sense goes back not just two or more centuries but two or more millennia. In the mythological terms of the age in which it first appeared, humanism is both Protean and Promethean—like Proteus it constantly changes its form, and like Prometheus it offers assistance to humanity and defiance to the gods. And in the philosophical terms of the age in which it first appeared, humanism involves both *philanthrôpia* and *paideia*—our identification with all other actual members of the human species, and our cultivation of the ideal humanity within ourselves and other men and women.

But *humanism* has been used in many other equally viable and valid senses, and we cannot claim any kind of ownership of or copyright in it; indeed the thousands of publications currently in print and the thousands of items currently on the Internet which use the word *humanism* still do so in dozens of different senses. It is up to us to show that our use of *humanism* is good enough for such a good word.

As a contribution to the common work toward this end, a one-man Manifesto of Modern Humanism is offered for the new millennium—not a minimum statement which humanists must accept, but an open-ended program from which humanists may take what they wish.

A Manifesto of Modern Humanism

Modern humanism is a system of belief and behavior based on the following assumptions, positive and negative:

Humanism, the axiomatic assumption of the primacy for human beings of human interests over all other interests, and of the primacy of what unites rather than what divides human beings—man is the measure of all things, all men and women are equal, though different from all other men and women. Human persons as autonomous indi-

viduals and the human species as a collective entity are more important than any particular intermediate human group or claim—family,
neighborhood, tribe, country, class, sect, caste, race, color, sex. All
human values are human creations. There is no evidence for any
superhuman beings or interests.

Freethought, the assumption of thought that is free and of freedom that
is thoughtful, and the assumption that this applies to others as much as
oneself.

Rationalism, the assumption of the primacy of reason over emotion, of
thought over feeling, of conscious over unconscious drives, alongside
the acceptance of the priority of emotion, feeling and unconscious
drives. Our reason tells us that our reason cannot tell us everything and
is the slave of our passions, and our rationality tests our irrationality.
There is no evidence that the heart has its reasons which reason does
not or cannot know.

Naturalism, the assumption that everything in the universe follows the
same regular patterns of existence, and that natural phenomena may
best be understood by the methods of science, based on observation
and hypothesis, verification or falsification, experiment and reason.
There is no evidence for any supernatural forces or powers.

Atheism, the assumption that there are no gods or goddesses, angels or
devils, ghosts or spirits, fairies or goblins, witches or wizards; and
agnosticism, the assumption that there are more things in heaven and
earth than are dreamt of in our philosophy, and that the universe is not
only queerer than we think but queerer than we can think.

Secularism, the assumption that this life and this world are all we
know and should care about, and that we should make the best of them
while we have the chance. There is no evidence for any other life after

or any other world beyond these ones, and even if there is, one world and one life at a time is quite enough.

Ethicism, the assumption of the moral and cooperative nature—alongside the immoral and competitive nature—of human beings, all originating in our genetic inheritance and developed by our cultural heritage, for us to make the best of ourselves. There is no evidence that we need outside assistance to be good or do right.

Aestheticism, the assumption of the artistic and creative nature of human beings—alongside the ugly and destructive nature—also originating in our genetic inheritance and developed by our cultural heritage, for us to make the finest of ourselves. There is no evidence that we need outside inspiration to seek or make beauty.

Eudemonism, the assumption that happiness is the only good. The overriding concern of private life should be to increase opportunities for happiness for oneself and one's fellows, and the overriding concern of public life should be to reduce the occasions of unhappiness for all. There is no evidence for any value higher than human happiness, but there is much evidence that true happiness is not found by directly seeking it.

Mutualism, the assumption that we should treat others as we wish others to treat us, respect our neighbors as ourselves, and treat humanity both in ourselves and in other human beings as an end in itself.

Realism, the assumption that we should be concerned with what is and can be rather than what we hope or fear may be. This involves pessimism of the intellect, the assumption that everything is as bad as it can be in the present world, and optimism of the will, the assumption that many things may be better in a future world, through our individual and collective effort.

Liberalism, the assumption that freedom is the highest political good; and *libertarianism*, the assumption that such freedom should be extended to the maximum extent compatible with the freedom of others.

Activism, the assumption that we should act to make life better for ourselves and others; and *quietism*, the assumption that the best form of action may be just to live and let live. The point is to understand the world before changing it, the task is to live in it as best we can, and the goal is to get the balance right.

Skepticism, the assumption that all these assumptions should be doubted, including this one.

Humorism, the assumption that life is a jest, and all things show it.

Note

The many publications about humanism the *thing* in all its many forms contain little reliable material about humanism the *word* in all its many senses, other than a few specialist monographs.

Most standard textbooks and reference books are either negatively uninformative or positively misinformative on the subject. Even the most reputable sources in English, such as the latest revised editions of the *Oxford English Dictionary* (1989) and the *Encyclopaedia Britannica* (1994), while they are necessary and useful starts, are incomplete and inaccurate guides, and other general dictionaries and encyclopedias are usually no better and frequently much worse. There are a few exceptions among recent American publications—*Encyclopedia of Philosophy* (1967), *Encyclopedia of Ethics* (1992), *International Encyclopedia of Ethics* (1995). Reference books are generally better in some other languages, and there are several excellent German examples.

There is little relevant material in publications by or studies of the freethought movement, even in specific studies of humanism, but there are some stimulating passages in David Tribe's *100 Years of Freethought* (1967) and *Nucleoethics* (1972), and there is much undigested information in Finngeir Hiorth's *Introduction to Humanism* (1996). The two American *Humanist Manifestos* have been reprinted together as a pamphlet, as has the *Secular Humanist Declaration* (both by Prometheus Books).

Harold Blackham's *Guide to Humanist Books in English* (*Plain View Supplement*, May 1955) is still the best general bibliography, though of course seriously out of date. Kwee Swan Liat's *Bibliography of Humanism* (1957), with Supplements, is very extensive but very unreliable.

Some standard books on modern humanism in English are as follows: Harold Blackham, *Humanism* (1968, 1976): second edition slightly revised. Julian Huxley, *The Humanist Frame* (1961), A. J. Ayer, *The Humanist Outlook* (1968), Paul Kurtz, *The Humanist Alternative* (1973): collections of various personal statements. Paul Kurtz, *In Defense of Secular Humanism* (1982): reprints *Humanist Manifesto II* and the *Secular Humanist Declaration*. Corliss Lamont, *Humanism as a Philosophy* (1949); *The Philosophy of Humanism* (1997): 8th edition, reprints the *Humanist Manifestos*. J. P. van Praag, *Foundations of Humanism* (1982): translation of 2d edition. M. N. Roy, *New Humanism* (1953): 2d edition.

The various humanist organizations around the world produce periodicals and many other publications, and there is also much humanist material on the Internet.

Index of Names